MY LIFE IN MUSIC

My Life in Music

Dame Fanny Waterman

Sir Alan.

A great friend of yours personally.

and I wish to help the Movement in any way.

FABER *ff* MUSIC

With gratitude — Dame Fanny

Consultant Editor: Wendy Thompson

© 2015 by Dame Fanny Waterman
First published in 2015 by Faber Music Ltd
Bloomsbury House, 74–77 Great Russell Street, London WC1B 3DA
Text Design by Agnesi Text, Hadleigh, Suffolk
Cover Design by Kenosha Design
Cover photographs by Geoffrey Raisman and Sheila Moulds
Printed and bound in England
by TJ International Ltd, Padstow, Cornwall

ISBN10: 0–571–53918–1
EAN13: 978–0–571–53918–5

This book is dedicated to

my dear husband
Geoffrey de Keyser

my sons
Robert and Paul

their families
Alex, Gemma, Lara, Tasha, Rosie and Carmella

my great grandsons
Leart, Sebastian and Zachary

and to my life-long friends
Karin Pfautsch and Joan Valentine OBE

I wish to acknowledge my gratitude to the many friends
who have supported and inspired me in the ninety-five years
over which this autobiography spans; it is impossible
to do justice to you all, but you know that you are loved
and cherished in my heart, and that you have my unending thanks
for your loyalty.

To Wendy Thompson for her brilliance, perception
and patience in capturing the many facets of my 'life tapestry'.
My publishers, Faber Music, in particular my editors
past and present, Martin Kingsbury, Kathryn Knight
and Lesley Rutherford.
To Professor Geoffrey Raisman and Sheila Moulds
for the charming cover photographs.

CONTENTS

PROLOGUE

I was speaking to Alan Bennett, one of our greatest writers, and told him that I was writing my autobiography. He said, 'Whatever you do, don't start at the beginning. Start in the middle.' So I thought back to the day my musical journey really began.

I was standing at a bus stop in Leeds on a summer's day in 1953 waiting for a bus to take me to Harrogate for a shopping expedition. I was really looking forward to it, as women do. Shopping can be very therapeutic. I was a housewife, married to a busy Leeds GP, with a three-year-old son, and for the past eight years or so I had been working as a piano teacher in Leeds.

I needed a hat to wear with a suit for a friend's wedding, and I pondered long and hard as to whether instead of green I should consider cream, which would match more outfits in my wardrobe. While I was thinking about this crucial decision, a car pulled over, and a friend of ours opened the door. He said, 'Can I give you a lift? Where are you going?' I said that I was going to Harrogate to shop, and he said, 'Well, jump in my car, as I'm going there to Sir John Barbirolli's rehearsal with the Hallé Orchestra. He's a great friend of mine. Do you want to come?' The name Barbirolli meant much more to me than going shopping, so I decided then and there to defer the important decision about the hat in favour of going to the rehearsal and meeting Sir John. He had been told about my pupil Allan Schiller, who had just caused quite a stir in Leeds playing the Haydn D major Concerto. After the rehearsal, I was introduced to Sir John. He fixed me with his piercing eyes and said, 'Could you prepare this boy to play the Mozart G major

Concerto K453 by the 6th of September at Leeds Town Hall with the Hallé?' Even though all Allan was learning at the time was a two-page Scarlatti sonata, I rashly plucked up my courage and said, 'Yes.' And that was a life-changing moment.

1

FROM RUSSIA TO LEEDS

All roads lead to Leeds, and all roads lead from Leeds.
FANNY WATERMAN

It was a bus, or rather a tram, that started my lifelong love affair with the piano. I was just a toddler, two years old, and my mother took me with her into Leeds when she went shopping. I listened to the rhythm that the tram wheels made, and squatted down on the floor, drumming the rhythm with my fingers. A passer-by saw me, and said to my mother, 'Your daughter is musical – you should get her some piano lessons!'

At that time, piano lessons must have seemed like an impossible luxury, as my parents were very impoverished. My father, Myer Wasserman, was born in 1892 in Berdichev, a city about 150 kilometres south-west of Kiev, in the Ukrainian district of Volhynia. I have never visited the city – I had a chance some years ago when I was invited to Kiev on the jury of the Horowitz Competition, and even though the current terrible violence hadn't yet erupted in Ukraine, we still had to be protected by people with guns. We were offered the opportunity to visit Berdichev, but my jury duties did not allow this and so took priority. I have always felt rather guilty that I never managed to visit my father's birthplace. I imagine the Berdichev of his childhood as the kind of place that Mussorgsky would have known and illustrated in his *Pictures from an Exhibition*, especially the musical portraits of the two Jews, one rich, one poor.

Berdichev lay on the edge of the so-called 'Pale of Settlement', the designated area on the western fringes of the Russian Empire

3

in which Jews were permitted to live. By 1870 about 46,000 of the population, some 80 per cent of the total, were Jewish. It was the second largest Jewish community in Russia and one of the most important in the whole of Eastern Europe. It was known as 'The Jerusalem of Volhynia', and had been home to one of the greatest Hassidic scholars and teachers, the famous Rebbe of Berdichev, the so-called 'Defender of the Jewish People'. As one of the centres of the Hassidic movement, Berdichev was a place where respected rabbis collected donations for the poor and preached the doctrine of 'love your neighbour'. People looked after one another.

Berdichev in the late nineteenth century was a hard-working city where most people made things, from clothes and upholstery to watches and jewellery. Like many Russian towns at that time, although deprived in some areas, it was a picturesque place, and my father recalled as a child how the streets turned into muddy swamps for many months of the year, especially when the winter snow melted. Most of the Yiddish-speaking population was very poor and barely literate. Jewish children were not allowed to attend regular Russian schools. Instead they went to elementary religious schools, where they were given a basic education in Hebrew, and studied Jewish history and commentaries on the Torah. My father probably attended one of these schools as a child, and his father, Mordecai Wasserman, taught Hebrew. He died when my father was seven years old.

The family had no carpets on the floors, just bare earth, and my father remembered that when one of his brothers or sisters died, there was no money for a coffin and the older children carried the body to its grave wrapped in a sheet. That must have happened often, as typhoid and tuberculosis were rampant in poor, over-crowded households. My father remembered his father travelling to Kiev to try to get a doctor for sick family members, and being very worried because Jews were not allowed into Kiev without a passport. And when the doctor did come, he required payment in advance. Because they had no money, the family hid his coat until he had treated the sick child.

We don't know exactly how many children my grandparents had, but it was a large family, and six children survived. The eldest, Chaim, went to university in Odessa, and then seems to have gone on to St Petersburg. He studied engineering, and stayed in Russia. He married and had children, and corresponded regularly with his brothers and sisters who had emigrated to England. His letters stopped some time during the Second World War, and we never found out what happened to him.

The rest of the Wasserman family all left Russia, probably as a result of the wave of vicious anti-Jewish pogroms that swept through the whole region. These pogroms – orgies of murder, looting and rape – had first started in 1881, after Jews were unjustly blamed for the assassination of Tsar Alexander II. The infamous so-called May Laws, brought in by the new Tsar in 1882, made life very harsh for the Jewish population. Jews lost the legal rights to their homes if they lived outside designated towns and *shtetls*. They were not allowed to trade on Sundays and Christian holidays, which, as they themselves could not trade on the Sabbath, reduced their working hours and their incomes. The Tsarist police enforced these new rules with great brutality, and systematically expelled Jewish families from small towns and villages. The press joined in the attacks. The head of the governing body of the Russian Orthodox Church said publicly that he hoped that 'one third of the Jews will convert, one third will die, and the rest will flee the country'.

These laws terrified the Jewish population, including my own family, who left in hope of finding a more safe and civilised life. They were wise to leave when they did. Just after the Russian Revolution, Berdichev suffered a terrible pogrom in which many people were killed. By the 1930s the city's Jewish population had dropped to around 31,000 and after the Germans invaded the Soviet Union in 1941, they confined the Jews to a ghetto. At the end of World War II there were no Jews left in Berdichev.

My father's elder brothers, Isaac and Nachman, and their sister Raisel, were the first to go. Isaac was a skilled tailor, and he made his way to England, to Leeds. Like Berdichev, Leeds was a city whose prosperity was founded in industry and commerce, especially the wool trade. From the nineteenth century onwards it began to attract immigrant Jewish workers, many from Russia and Poland. One of these was Michael Marks, the son of a Polish tailor. In 1884 he set up a trestle table in Kirkgate Market selling many goods for a penny. His famous 'Penny Bazaar' has grown into the iconic British firm of Marks & Spencer. Then came the entrepreneur of Lithuanian origin, Montague Burton. Leeds benefited not only from Montague's commercial acumen, which created jobs, but also from his philanthropy – he endowed several buildings in the University. His son Stanley carried on his father's work – he and his wife Audrey were great benefactors to the cultural life of Leeds as well as close personal friends.

The Jewish community of Leeds, which was the third largest in the British Isles, continued to expand. By the time that Isaac, Nachman and Raisel Wasserman arrived, it had reached a high point of about 22,000. They were of course lost in their new environment, and we still have an English–Yiddish phrase-book that my family all used. One of the phrases is 'Can you tell me where is the station for Leeds?' Many of the Jewish families in Leeds worked in the clothing trade, and lived near the factories. Isaac and Nachman set up a tailoring business, and my Aunt Raisel was their seamstress.

In 1909 my grandmother and her two youngest children – my father Myer and his sister Tillie – took the boat from Bremerhaven and landed in Hull, before travelling to join the rest of the family in Leeds. At first my father was expected to join his brothers in the tailoring business, but his talent lay in other areas. This turned out to be in the jewellery business, where he developed a vast knowledge and understanding of diamonds. He could barely speak a few words of English – Yiddish stayed his main language throughout his life. I can remember him trying to play charades, and struggling with the English titles of films. He once tried to do *The Constant Nymph*, and kept pointing to his foot – all he could think of was the word 'corn', which he thought sounded like 'con'. Like his elder brothers, he decided to Anglicise his surname, as many Jewish families did once they had settled in England. He wrote his new English name in his phrase-book – Meyer Voter-mann – which was how he pronounced Waterman.

By 1915 he found lodgings in Adler Street, a street that runs between Whitechapel Road and Commercial Road in the heart of London's old Jewish East End. Adler Street was named after the pioneering Yiddish actor Jacob Adler, who came to London from Odessa and became an actor in the East End in the 1880s. He established a Yiddish theatre there – the Grand Palais, which became famous. After toiling for long hours in the sweatshops, the workers loved to go to the theatre and hear their mother tongue. The East End at that time was a desperately poor and overcrowded place, and my father must have been horrified by the squalor he found there, much worse than at home in Russia. When Jacob Adler had arrived twenty or so years earlier, he wrote:

> The further we penetrated into Whitechapel, the more our hearts sank. Was this London? Never in Russia, never later in the worst slums of New York, were we to see such poverty as in the London of the 1880s.

The writer Jack London left a vivid description of the humiliating poverty suffered by the East End's inhabitants, whom he called 'The People of the Abyss':

> At a market, tottery old men and women were searching in the garbage thrown in the mud for rotten potatoes, beans and vegetables, while little children clustered like flies around a festering mass of fruit, thrusting their arms to the shoulders into the liquid corruption, and drawing forth morsels but partially decayed, which they devoured on the spot . . .

Then came the First World War. By the summer of 1915 the East End was being hit by occasional Zeppelin bombing raids. My father couldn't stand the noise, and within a few months he was back with his family in Leeds. By then he was aged twenty-two and must have felt that he was doing well enough to consider getting married. In Leeds he met Mary Behrman, the daughter of Russian emigrant Jews. Her parents, Solomon Behrman and Fanny Silverman, lived at 9 Rockingham Street, in an industrial area in the city centre. Solomon worked as a slipper-makers' machinist, but by 1901 he had gone up in the world, and was giving his occupation as 'portrait painter'. He did in fact hand-tint photographs! By then Fanny had given birth to two daughters, my mother Mary in 1891 and her younger sister Rebecca two years later, and the family had moved to 64 Albert Grove, in an area of Headingley known as 'Little London'. Many Jewish families lived there, and I can remember that the street also contained the Jewish Women's Public Baths. In 1906 the family had a late addition, another daughter called Bessie. At some point after that Solomon decided that Leeds was not good enough for him, and he took off to Paris to pursue his dream of becoming a painter, abandoning his wife and children. So after my mother and father were married at the New Briggate Synagogue on 17 October 1915, they decided to stay in Leeds, rather than return to London. My father found work, eventually opening his own jeweller's business, and moved into 64 Albert Grove to live with his wife's family. And it was in that grim street of back-to-back houses that my brother Harry was born in 1917, and I was born on 22 March 1920, and named after my grandmother.

2

CHILDHOOD

Both Harry and I grew up knowing that our family didn't have much money. As a young child, I remember sitting in the damp basement kitchen at 64 Albert Grove. It didn't have a window at ground level and you couldn't see the sky, just pairs of shoes walking up and down outside. One of my earliest memories is of my father getting up very early in the morning and poking the embers in the grate to light the fire in the kitchen so that Harry and I would be warm before we left for school. There were anxious times, too, when there wasn't enough money to pay the grocer. But I was a contented child with a supportive family, and I remember us all sitting round the kitchen table listening to Henry Hall and the BBC Dance Orchestra on the radio, especially when they played songs like 'Here Comes the Bogeyman', 'The Teddy Bears' Picnic' and 'Here's to the Next Time'. I liked to waltz round the table to the Dance Orchestra. On Saturday afternoons we were sometimes given a twopenny Cadbury's chocolate bar each and taken to the cinema. I remember seeing Laurel and Hardy trying to get an upright piano into a room on the second floor of a house and blaming each other – 'A fine mess you've got me into!' – and Charlie Chaplin in *City Lights* waiting for a young, pretty girl to join him, but she doesn't come. That made me cry. I loved those films. They moved me much more than anything that's on the TV today.

On sunny days in the summer we took the tram from the bottom of the road to Roundhay Park. We didn't have enough money for deckchairs, but we sat on the grass listening to the band playing 'I Do Like To Be Beside the Seaside' and other popular hits. There was a regular troupe of seven pierrots at the bandstand. They were a group of people who sang popular songs of the day, and I thought it was marvellous. And at the end they held up the letters C-H-E-E-R-I-O, one each, and sang 'Cheerio, everybody, cheerio', and then, from being out in the sunshine, we had to get back into the tramcar and go back to the dismal house in Albert Grove. Those outings were a real treat.

The house we lived in was small and cramped, and for the first ten years of my life we shared it with my Aunt Bessie. In 1930 my father's youngest sister Aunt Tillie left Leeds to live in America, so there is now an American branch of the family, and my cousin still writes to me. Sometimes our Uncle Nachman came to visit. He was married to Auntie Sossie, but they had no children. I remember being very nervous of her – because she appeared to have a moustache! We were all rather afraid of her – she used to come and stand over my mother in the kitchen while she was cooking. One day my mother was experimenting with a new electric stove. Things were not going well, and there was a terrible smell of burning. Auntie Sossie said to my mother, 'But surely there must be a Book of Destruction?' She went on to say that her friend had a gas cooker that had two 'gorillas'!

Uncle Nachman and Auntie Sossie enjoyed playing a card game called Solo, for four people. One day my mother picked up what they called a wonderful hand for making tricks – the Ace, King, Queen, Jack and ten of trumps – and she held it tightly to her chest so that no one could overlook what she was going to do. She didn't start leading from the Ace but from the lower card, and worked her way up with a beaming smile of achievement. At the post-mortem there was a heated discussion as to why she had done that, and she said triumphantly, 'Actually, I did that to mislead you!' At which point Auntie Sossie said, 'Nachman, get your coat, we're going!' They left, and didn't come back for twenty years.

My father was typically 'Yiddishkeit' – he was sarcastic and funny. He would ask me, 'So vot is in the news?' I would tell him, and he would shrug and say, 'So vot?' His political views were very left-wing. He had no nostalgia for his early life in Russia. He realised early on that life, though still hard, was better in England. In Russia, if you had no money, there was nothing to eat. I remember my aunt Raisel saying, 'I'd not seen a chicken until I came to England!' In my childhood, my family observed Jewish religious practice. We ate kosher food, we kept traditional Friday night dinner, and we observed the principal Jewish festivals – Rosh Hashanah (New Year), Yom Kippur (the Day of Atonement, the most solemn day in the Jewish calendar), Hanukkah (the Festival of Lights), and Pesach (Passover). The only tradition that my father could not observe was that of not working on a Saturday. He had his business and his shop to run, and could not afford not to open on Saturdays.

My father worked mainly in platinum and gold. I remember watching him with his tweezers handling little rubies, diamonds and sapphires, and making his own designs that were favoured by the great jewellery firms, and by the people who could afford them. He was really an artist. But although he was a jeweller, dealing in luxury goods, the works of art he created were much more impor-tant to him than the money he made out of them, which wasn't much. If he didn't like the look of a customer, he wouldn't even open up his safe to show them what was available. He told my brother and myself not to accept flattery from people and to judge people only by their actions, not what they say. He was so right. My brother and I were taught never to value material things, but instead to value good health, beauty, talent, reliability and integrity. Those values were part of our lives. I've always placed a high value on trust and loyalty, and all through my life I've chosen my friends with that in mind.

My mother was very well read. After I started school I remem-ber her kneeling on a chair (she always knelt, rather than sitting), reading wonderful books to me – *Black Beauty*, *Little Women*, *The Mill on the Floss*, Dickens. The description of the drowning of Steerforth in *David Copperfield* made me cry, as did the end of *The Mill on the Floss* when Maggie and Tom Tulliver die in the flood and are buried under a headstone inscribed 'In death they were not divided'. Certain words and phrases as expressed by the great writers have as much emotional power over me as Beethoven's late masterpieces. If my mother came across a passage that she thought was particularly memorable, she would say, 'Listen to this, Fanny, and remember it', and I often managed to get the same phrases into my English essays at school – whether they were appropriate or not. I started one such essay with the rather grandiose phrase 'What is more enjoyable than the holiday itself is the week of anticipation preceding it', and the teacher announced, 'Pens down, girls, listen to how Fanny Waterman has started her composition!'

My primary school days were some of the happiest of my life. When I was five I went to Cowper Street Primary School in Chapeltown. At school I learned that one of the most important rules in life was to be punctual. One of my great friends, Joan Valentine, who was at school with me, and became Head Girl, instilled in me the importance of 'Better three hours too soon than a minute too late', as Shakespeare said. Joan was three years older than me. She was one of the greatest influences on my life apart from my parents and, of course, my husband Geoffrey. Joan was immaculate in her style and behaviour. She became a teacher, and then a headmistress herself, at a poor school in Armley – the sort of school when on the days when there was a hanging at Armley Gaol, the children turned up late because they'd all gone off to see the announcement posted that the man had been executed – it was the main event of their day. Later she became Principal of St John's College in York. She still had time for me after she retired – she called me her 'Retirement Charity'! She was an invaluable help to us with the Leeds Piano Competition. I can see her now, typing out my dictated letters on an old typewriter with carbon paper, and with never a mistake. She used *Debrett's Style Manual* to check that everyone had been correctly addressed according to their station and profession, and took great care not to offend anyone.

When I went to school, I used to giggle a lot. They say giggling is the only genuine laughter. I remember having a fit of giggles after shaking a daffodil and the water dripped off the petals on to the desk. The exasperated mistress said, 'Fanny Waterman, come out here! If you don't stop giggling, I'm going to put your head in a bucket of cold water!' I took this to heart. I was so ashamed that I burst into tears in front of the class. I had displayed a terrible lack of judgement for laughing at something so trivial, and that disgraceful episode never left my memory. Teachers should be respected. After your parents, they are the best friends you will ever have. Children should have that impressed upon them from their earliest days.

By the time I was seven or eight, my parents had moved to their own house, in Gathorne Terrace in the Chapeltown district of Leeds. They bought a battered old out-of-tune upright piano, and installed it in the front room. I began to learn the piano, and Harry the violin. There was no really good piano teacher available locally. My first teacher, Mrs Goldstone, kept her piano in the kitchen, and gave me lessons whilst preparing her husband's dinner. I'm not sure she could even read music. She used to feed me stale bits of cake to keep me going, and left me plodding through 'Pixies on Parade', 'In a Monastery Garden', and 'Tiptoe Through the Tulips' while she got on with cooking and washing up. I hope her culinary powers were better than her piano teaching – I can still smell her food! But my parents didn't seem to have the courage to say 'enough is enough'. Then I tried another teacher – a man this time – but all I remember is having a lesson in the basement of his music shop, and he put his arm round me. I told my parents I didn't want to be taught by him, but I couldn't say why.

Harry's violin teacher was a man called Arthur W. Kaye, who lived on Lord Street in Huddersfield. I used to go with Harry to his lessons, to accompany him on the piano, and Mr Kaye introduced us to the chamber music repertoire. He was a very knowledgeable musician, and I looked forward to the lessons – Arthur Kaye taught me as much about music as anyone else. Those lessons were the foundation of my musicianship.

When I was eleven, four girls were chosen from the elementary school to try for a scholarship to Leeds Girls' High School and I was one of them. They interviewed the parents, and called my mother in – I remember her going off in a shabby old maroon coat. The school was very posh and we never had a reply as to whether I had been accepted or rejected. So I didn't get the scholarship and my mother always blamed herself that she let me down. I think she practically had a nervous breakdown about it.

Instead, I was given a scholarship to Chapel Allerton High School, which was a kind of sister institution to Leeds Girls' High – we wore the same green uniforms. The headmistress, Miss Scotson Clark, was about to retire, but she interviewed all the forthcoming pupils. She asked me what my father's occupation was, because most of the girls' fathers were doctors, solicitors, or other middle-class professional people, and when I said, 'He makes jewellery', she curled her lip, lifted up her eyes to heaven, and said, 'Oh, in *trade*!' I still remember the deep feeling of humiliation. However, her successor, Norah J. Henderson, was a major influence on my life. She liked to deliver daily homilies at morning assembly, and exhorted us always 'to do better than our best'. The school motto was *In minimis fidelis*, a quotation from St Luke's Gospel which translates as 'Be faithful in little things'. Norah Henderson's favourite sayings, such as 'Whatever you do, you must do to the best of your ability', or 'You've always got to aim to be better than the best, and try harder', left a great impression on me, and my own life has been guided by many of the maxims which I learned at school.

I liked poetry, and I had a very good English mistress. I remember our class being asked to explain the phrase 'The child is father to the man' from the Wordsworth poem 'My Heart Leaps Up'. I was the only one at the time who really understood its meaning: that what we do as children will inform our later lives. I wasn't any good at sciences, though, or geography. If I didn't like the teacher, I didn't try very hard at the subject. I also learned French when I was at school, and later on, when I was in the sixth form, the teacher said, 'You should learn German if you're going to be a musician.' How right she was. When I'm on an international jury, I can often make myself understood with a bit of pidgin German, and of course, German is so important for understanding many directions in musical scores.

In spite of the inadequacies of my first piano teacher, I had made good progress on the piano, and was already one of the most promising pianists in the school. So I was asked to play at morning assembly. I quickly learned many of the hymns in *Ancient and Modern*, and playing all those beautiful hymns really improved my singing tone on the piano. It was a great thrill to be playing there, to feel I was wanted, instead of just 'the daughter of Someone in Trade'. Miss Henderson always had a beautiful smile for me and she always waited for me to play the Lord's Prayer. She said when she heard me after the girls had marched out, 'You make me cry when you play that.' But at first I wasn't too popular with the other girls. Invitations to parties were passed round to everyone in the class – except me. I was devastated. I took a long look at myself, and wondered why, until I realised that if I wanted to be invited, I had better stop talking about Bach, Beethoven and Brahms, and meet the other girls on their own terms. So I learned to play all the popular songs of the 1930s, and from then on, I was much in demand at parties. One of my girlhood dreams was to be well liked and popular. Has this dream come true?

My parents did their best for my musical education. They took me to concerts to hear Cortot, Kreisler, Heifetz and Schnabel if they came to play in Leeds. I also remember going to hear Rachmaninov play at Leeds Town Hall. He was a very tall man, well over six feet, gaunt and unsmiling, with bags under his eyes. He stared at the audience and then sat down to play with just a little pool of light on the piano. We all sat in silence like statues. The first piece he played was the Bach B flat Partita.

On reflection, I don't think my parents were very good psychologists. I didn't work very hard as a child, and I was always being compared unfavourably to Harry, who did work hard. I had to be reminded about practising, whereas Harry was quite different. But I think now that you shouldn't weigh and compare your own children's talents. When I was fifteen, in October 1935, Harry and I took part in the sonata class at the Blackpool Music Festival. We played one of the most difficult Mozart violin sonatas, and the adjudicator was Dr Herbert Howells. In his adjudication, he said:

They were brother and sister in movement, as well as other-wise. Fanny treated the piano like a box of toys, inviting Harry to gaily join in the fun. She shaped things . . . The decisive and gifted work of the pianist was constantly giving her a superiority of interest, but there was a family disagreement at the top of page three.

After I left school at seventeen I was heard by Dr Herbert Thompson, the distinguished music critic of the *Yorkshire Post*. He wrote to Myra Hess after hearing me play, and said that I had the makings of a great artist and could she hear me? She replied that she was working 25 hours a day, and was too busy – which I now appreciate! – but that the best thing would be if I was auditioned by her teacher, Tobias Matthay. Matthay was quite a controversial figure – but he was said to be one of the best piano teachers working in Britain, and his manual on piano teaching, *The Art of Touch*, was very influential. So many students wanted to study with him that in 1905 he had opened his own piano school, which was based in his London house at 94 Wimpole Street. As a teacher, he stressed the importance of touch and arm movements. He also taught at the Royal Academy of Music, but in 1925 the Principal there, who had been one of his own pupils, publicly attacked his teaching methods and Matthay was forced to resign his professorship at the Academy. Nevertheless he produced some marvellous students, such as Myra Hess, Clifford Curzon, Harriet Cohen and Moura Lympany.

When my father took me to see Matthay, he said, 'Where did you come from?' I said that my father was a Russian Jew, and he said, 'There's nothing greater than a Russian Jew, they are marvellous musicians.' When you think about it, so many of the greatest ones were. Matthay's fee was two guineas for half an hour, three guineas for three-quarters of an hour and four for an hour. We couldn't afford anything more than two guineas, and I'll never forget at five o'clock in the morning hearing the rumbling of the tram at the bottom of the road that would take me to Leeds Station to catch the train to London for my half-hour lesson. The train fare cost ten and sixpence, and my father told me, 'A man can keep a wife and family for a week on what I'm giving you.' I don't remember being given any sandwiches, just a packet of peanuts to keep me going. In my lessons with Matthay we concentrated on interpretation rather than technique, especially phrasing, pedalling and rubato. He used to say, 'When you perform, the music must never stand still except in pause or rest, it should always move forward and flow.' I don't remember a great deal about my lessons with him, but I certainly must have learnt something.

3

FROM LEEDS TO LONDON

For my eighteenth birthday my father bought me my own piano. It was a second-hand Steinway grand which cost £99.99 – a huge sum in those days – and it took up nearly all the front room of our house. My father wanted me to be surrounded by people who inspired me, and if he met anyone who was musical or artistic, he would invite them to the house. We had musical evenings when I played on my own, or else piano trios and quartets with other people. And I also started giving lessons myself, to earn pocket money, as well as giving concerts.

I remember having a dress made at around that time. It was meant to be something 'neat, clean and tidy', suitable for everyday wear. I returned home with it to show my mother, but when I unwrapped it, her face froze. It was so garish. It was made of red wool georgette, with a sunray pleated skirt, assorted coloured beading, and a velvet trim. It made me look like a Christmas tree. My mother swallowed hard and said, so as not to upset me, 'Well, you can always wear it "up" for everyday!'

In February 1941 I had my first chance to play a Mozart concerto with the Leeds Symphony Orchestra at the Town Hall. Three months later I won the Mathilde Verne Scholarship to the Royal College of Music. I was taught by Cyril Smith, who was one of the great English pianists. Looking back I think that perhaps he wasn't appreciated or recognised enough. People with foreign names like Solomon were all the rage at that time. Cyril taught me to look at music accurately, because until then I tended to be sloppy. I was probably playing a lot of wrong notes and not scrutinising the score. Like Joan Valentine and my headmistress Miss Henderson, Cyril Smith taught me to become a perfectionist. You need someone like that to stop you becoming complacent about your own playing, and to encourage you to strive to reach their own high standard. I would go and listen to Cyril at his rehearsals, and I heard him playing Rachmaninov's Third Concerto, which is one of the most difficult piano concertos. At that time it wasn't often played. The next morning I had a lesson. I remember standing on the doorstep ringing the bell and hearing him practising, very, very slowly, just one simple part of the Rachmaninov that obviously hadn't satisfied him. That extraordinary attention to detail made me realise how essential very slow practice is. Cyril Smith had a great sense of humour. He once told us that he had been practising the Rachmaninov Third Concerto in an empty hall in preparation for his concert. When he paused to wipe his brow, he overheard two cleaners talking. One said to the other, 'I bet that piano player hasn't done a decent day's work in his life!'

By then the Blitz had started, so instead of living in London I went to live in Oxford, at the suggestion of a student friend, Gershon Avner, who was then President of the Oxford Union. I travelled up to London for lessons twice a week. I did enjoy the musical life in Oxford. It was such a beautiful environment, and I sang madrigals with the girls who were at Somerville College. But I had to live in digs, and I had some very odd experiences. The problem with being a pianist, rather than a violinist or a singer, for example, is that you need a piano on which to practise. I started off in digs with a Mrs Mendelsohn, and her house was so cold, especially the bedroom. I remembered the story about Marie Curie, when she was living in lodgings, putting chairs on top of the bed to give her a little extra warmth, so I did the same, but with no success. I cried all night, and wrote to Cyril Smith telling him that I wanted to go home. I was so homesick. I still have the letter he wrote me, saying, 'Take heart, and come and see me as soon as possible.' I didn't go home, but instead I moved on to live in a very nice house, owned by a woman who liked to show me her clothes. She showed me all her beautiful lacy nightdresses, which I thought were lovely. I was very envious. But then I began to notice that the doorbell rang a lot, the door used to open and close every half hour or so, and some American soldiers used to come and go. Meanwhile, I continued to practise. Whatever was going on, it was none of my business. But eventually I realised that I was living in a brothel!

In August 1942 I was asked to join my fellow students Colin Horsley and Joan Baker in a performance of Bach's Triple Concerto No. 2 in C at the Proms, which were now taking place in the Albert Hall after the Queen's Hall had been bombed. There was a note at the bottom of the programme, which read:

> In the event of an Air Raid warning, the audience will be informed immediately, so that those who wish to take shelter, either in the building or in the public shelters outside, may do so. The concert will then continue.

Fortunately, ours was not interrupted! Afterwards I received a personal letter from Sir Henry Wood, thanking me for my 'excellent performance' of the Bach concerto. 'The ensemble was fine, & thanks to the keen interest you all took in the Concerto and the amount of time you gave to its rehearsal, the work created a deep impression'. I still have that letter, framed on the wall.

In my last term at the Royal College of Music in 1943 I won two prizes, the Challen & Sons Gold Medal and the Ellen Shaw Williams Prize. The prizes were presented by the young Princess Elizabeth – it was her first public engagement. She must have been only seventeen. She gave me my medals and said to me, 'Congratulations, you have been most successful.' Seventy years later I had the honour of sitting next to Her Majesty the Queen at a lunch in honour of her visit to Leeds on the occasion of her Diamond Jubilee. I reminded her that she presented me with a medal on her first visit as President to the Royal College of Music, and that I recalled that she was accompanied by an aged lady-in-waiting. The Queen immediately replied, 'But she wasn't aged at all!' I never imagined that seventy years on I would find myself sitting at the same lunch table as the Queen. The road I have travelled is always full of unexpected turns. One can never take anything for granted.

In the spring of 1943 I was due to be called up for war service in the Women's Land Army. I knew I would be no good at all with a spade, but Sir George Dyson, the Principal of the College, told me that teaching was a reserved occupation which would exempt me from national service. So I opted for that. I left the RCM with glowing testimonials. Cyril Smith called me 'a brilliantly gifted pianist and musician who will be a source of inspiration to her pupils'.

I applied to teach in a boarding school in Eltham. Teachers and pupils alike there were very badly treated. One of my young fellow teachers, a girl called Else Hoxter, used to come into my room at night to chat about music. The headmistress, a Miss Berry, took a very dim view of that, telling us our relationship was 'unhealthy'. We were expected to look after the children first thing in the mornings before breakfast, and then to spend our weekends writing reports on our pupils' progress, but then we found that Miss Berry was rewriting them to flatter the parents, and was being economical with the truth. When I complained about the extra weekend work, Miss Berry said to me, 'Miss Waterman, if I had known that you wanted so much time off, I would never have appointed you.' I drew myself up and replied, 'Miss Berry, if I had known that I had not only to teach music, but also be a nursemaid to unhappy children from broken marriages, I would never have accepted the job.' So I left, and went back to Leeds, where I was immediately offered a post teaching the piano at my old school.

4

MARRIAGE

Back in September 1941, when I was giving a recital in the Leeds Art Gallery just before I was due to go back to London after the summer holidays, I had been introduced to a young medical student called Geoffrey de Keyser. Geoffrey was three years younger than me. He came from London, where his father was a senior civil servant in the Board of Trade. The de Keyser family was also Jewish, originally from Lithuania and Latvia. Geoffrey's younger brother, David, has had a successful career as an actor in film, television, and on stage – he played the psychiatrist opposite Frances de la Tour in Tom Kempinski's play *Duet for One*, based on the tragedy of Jacqueline du Pré. But Geoffrey decided to follow a medical career. He was the only student in his year to win an open scholarship to the Middlesex Hospital Medical School, but like many other medical students in wartime he had been evacuated to a provincial hospital – in his case the Leeds General Infirmary – after the Middlesex was damaged by enemy bombing in September 1940.

The recital was on a Wednesday, and on Friday I was introduced to Geoffrey by a mutual friend. I was very taken with him: he was very charming and such a handsome young man – a real Adonis! We found we had much in common, especially music. Geoffrey was really passionate about it. A few days later he visited me again, saying he'd forgotten his pen! I think about a week passed, and we went out to the cinema together. A short time later, after our friendship was strengthening, he mentioned the idea of our getting married, and asked if I might consider moving to London. I thought that was a marvellous idea, but Geoffrey's parents had just separated, and he was in a state of shock. Geoffrey's father, however, did say that he would give us his blessing in three years' time, after Geoffrey had qualified, if at that time we still felt the same way about each other.

By the time I returned to Leeds in 1944, we couldn't bear to be apart any longer. Geoffrey and I were married on 16 August 1944 at the Beth Hamedrash Synagogue in Leeds. There were only about twenty-four people at the ceremony, owing to the war, and the recent separation of Geoffrey's parents. It was a very simple wedding, as neither of us had any money, and he wasn't yet fully qualified as a doctor. On the morning of the wedding, the headmistress of the school where I taught, Norah Henderson, said that she had never been to a Jewish wedding, and that she would love to come and bring some of her staff, who were then my colleagues. We made them very welcome, although I was worried about Auntie Sossie. I didn't want my simple Russian auntie, whose English was poor, to start a conversation with the headmistress. But I needn't have been so embarrassed. When I looked up, I was relieved to see Miss Henderson looking as if she was interested in every word Auntie Sossie had to say. After the ceremony, Miss Henderson said to me, 'Where is your bridegroom?' I didn't know, so we looked for him, and found him lying in the grass reading a book. Geoffrey was never without a book in his hand, even on our wedding day!

At first, the circumstances of our married life weren't easy. We had to divide our time between a tiny hospital flat in Ashford, Kent, where Geoffrey was a registrar, and my parents' home in Leeds. When Geoffrey qualified in 1945, he expected to be called up straight away and sent abroad, but on the day he passed his finals, the war in Europe ended. That was an eventful day for him. He was having a celebratory tea with his mother in a Lyons Corner House, when someone at the next table took out a gun and shot his whole family. When the police arrived, Geoffrey went to the door to let them in and explain what had happened, but when he finally returned to his table, he was dismayed to find that his mother had calmly finished his ice-cream!

In 1949 he was called up for National Service in the Royal Army Medical Corps, where he rose to the rank of major and served in Egypt, so we were often separated for long periods. But after his discharge, he decided to look for a job in general practice in Leeds, so that was where we settled. In 1950 Geoffrey became a GP at a practice in Morley, a small textile town a few miles southeast of the city. When he first arrived in Morley, there were 57 working mills recycling yarn from old rags, and there was a terrible stench – Geoffrey said you could taste the fumes in the air. The senior partner in the practice wanted us to go and live there, but I had strong misgivings. I felt that there was not enough music there to nourish me, and that we would be much better living in Leeds. Nevertheless Morley was a very friendly town, and Geoffrey stayed there for the rest of his working life, eventually becoming senior partner of the practice himself, chairman of the Leeds Medical Committee, and a member of the management board of the Leeds Western Health Authority. He was very popular with his patients – he called them 'the salt of the earth'. He was a fierce champion of the new post-war National Health Service, and fought tenaciously for people to have access to clean air and water – as well as free birth control. There was still a great deal of poverty in northern industrial areas in those post-war years, and Geoffrey was always very concerned for his patients' wellbeing. He would even make his elderly patients a cup of tea when he visited them.

The practice prospered, and in later years, Geoffrey's patients were surprised and quite amused to see their GP turning up for home visits in a Rolls-Royce! Geoffrey was a real car enthusiast. We first bought a 1955 R-type Bentley, and he spent many Saturday afternoons in overalls lying on his back underneath the car, de-carbonising it. Later on we exchanged it for a Rolls-Royce Silver Shadow.

During the early years of our marriage, while Geoffrey was away on National Service in Egypt, I continued my professional playing career. In 1944 I joined up with another Leeds-based musician, the violinist Rosemary Rapaport. Rosemary had been a student at

My father and mother

My parents' wedding photo

My father making a carriage   Myself as a young child

With Rosemary Rapaport (left), my sonata partner and founder
of the Purcell School of Music (of which I am still a Patron)

Myself in concert dress, aged twenty-one (opposite page)

My wedding day

Geoffrey de Keyser, aged eighteen

Allan Schiller and Sir John Barbirolli

My early pupils: Allan Schiller, Kathleen Jones, Michael Roll and Wendy Waterman

Kathleen Jones   With Terence Judd

Teaching Michael Roll

At the piano with Erich Gruenberg

In my kitchen!

At home with Geoffrey and sons Paul and Robert

the Royal Academy of Music, but she and her husband, who was also her agent, lived for a while in Leeds. Rosemary was a very lively girl in more ways than one. She had originally been engaged to her future son-in-law, but then married his father instead. Her husband was quite a lot older than she was, and I think she probably married him because she thought he could help her with her career. After the war they moved back to London. She had always had a dream to start a specialist music school, and in 1962 she set up what eventually became the Purcell School. I was one of the school's first patrons.

While we were playing together as a duo, Rosemary and I gave many concerts at music clubs and societies all over the north of England. We specialised in the central works of the sonata repertoire, especially Beethoven, Mozart and Brahms, which intensified my lifelong love of chamber music – a love that had begun much earlier as a result of my contact with Harry's violin teacher Arthur Willie Kaye, and which formed the basis of my musical development. My solo career also continued to flourish. In December 1947 I gave a recital in Leeds, which was broadcast by the BBC and repeated three months later, and I was also taken on by the prestigious London concert agency of Ibbs & Tillett, then managed by the formidable Emmie Tillett, the so-called 'Duchess of Wigmore Street', who did so much to promote the careers of many great musicians. I began to get more concerto dates – at the end of 1948 I played Mozart's 'Coronation' Concerto with the BBC Northern Orchestra in Manchester under Charles Groves. That concert was broadcast, and more followed, including an all-Bach recital for the Third Programme in February 1948 and a performance of Beethoven's Second Piano Concerto with the BBC Northern Orchestra under Groves in April 1949. And in 1950 I took part in a series of concerts in Leeds Parish Church (now Leeds Minster) for the 200th anniversary of Bach's death, playing the Bach D minor Concerto. I recently returned there for a dear friend, Victor Watson's memorial service, and reflected that 65 years ago, I had performed in that very church. So much has happened in my life since then.

Not long after that concert, our first son Robert was born in February 1950. He had asthma as a child, and we were very worried about his health – we could hear him wheezing at night through the bedroom door. So I decided that for a while at least I should devote myself to motherhood. By then we had moved into a house called Sunway, off King Lane in Moortown. It was a detached house, with a drawing room big enough to take two pianos, and we had many enjoyable musical evenings there. So between us we were progressing in both our professions: Geoffrey's practice was building up, and I decided to concentrate on my teaching career, as well as looking after Robert and his younger brother Paul, who arrived in 1956. At various times since then, some of our musical friends suggested that we might do better to go to live in London, and occasionally I was tempted, but Geoffrey stalwartly refused to live anywhere other than Leeds. It was a reversal of our previous roles, when I had wanted to stay in Leeds and he had wanted to move to London.

Without Geoffrey I wouldn't have achieved anything. We shared the bonds of love and music. There couldn't be a better basis for a marriage. He was always very proud and very supportive of my musical endeavours. Of course he wasn't a professional musician, and I'm not sure that he realised the real depth of my musicianship – sometimes he seemed rather bemused that people such as Benjamin Britten treated what I had to say with so much respect! But Geoffrey's knowledge of music, opera in particular, far surpassed mine. He could deliver lectures to musical organisations – from memory – on a wide range of pieces, from Beethoven's Ninth Symphony to Strauss's *Der Rosenkavalier*, which made a great impression. His memory was simply phenomenal.

He told me he loved me practically every day. One day, anticipating a compliment, I challenged him and asked him, 'Why?' To which he replied, 'Because you are so unpredictable!' Sometimes I would shout 'Geoffrey!' and he would simply respond with one word, 'Busy!' And that meant he wasn't to be disturbed.

Geoffrey and I were once invited to stay at the Mansion House by Sir Christopher Walford, the Lord Mayor of London. We were attending a small formal party at which the Prime Minister, John Major, was present. The Prime Minister said to Geoffrey, 'I know what your wife does, but tell me, what do *you* do?' Geoffrey replied, 'Well, I'm a retired GP and a member of the Consort Club.' 'How interesting!' said the Prime Minister. 'I've never heard of the Consort Club. Do tell me about it.' 'Well,' said Geoffrey, 'when I tell you that the other two members are Denis Thatcher and the Duke of Edinburgh, need I say more?' To which John Major replied, 'Now I understand! But whatever has happened to *them?*'

Geoffrey and I were together for 60 years and married for 57. Our Golden Wedding anniversary was a quiet occasion. We didn't have a big party – it was just the two of us. He asked me, 'Are you bored with me, darling?' And I said, 'Not at all. Are you bored with me?' At which he just went on reading!

5

PRODIGIES AND PARENTS

I had really taken to piano teaching. Miss Henderson, who had been my headmistress when I was at school, was still at Allerton High School when I became a teacher there. I had about forty pupils, as many as I could manage. I had been entering them for Associated Board exams, and many of them were getting distinctions. Inevitably I did have some who were less successful – I have kept a letter dated May 1945 from one parent who wrote:

> Dear Madam
>
> To my way of thinking one must love music in order to excel in it. The same, I suppose, applies to any other subject.
>
> It appears to me that Doreen is rather indifferent to her music, seeing that she has to be reminded nearly every time to go to the piano.
>
> I shall be very greateful [sic] to have your advise [sic] if under the circumstances it is worth for her to continue taking music lessons.
>
> I beg to assure you that I am well aware of the enormous progress Doreen made under your instructions; but for the last few weeks she became very slack in her music practise at home.

Fortunately, not all my pupils were like Doreen, and over the next few years I found I had a waiting list. One day, the doorbell rang. It was a local lady called Mrs Schiller, who asked me if I could teach her son Allan. He had started the piano at six, and was then aged eight. I took him on as a private pupil.

Allan made exceptionally good progress, and in the spring of 1953 he played Haydn's D major Piano Concerto at a concert in Leeds. Reports of this performance had come to the attention of Sir John Barbirolli, whom I met in Harrogate on that momentous afternoon when I decided to abandon my quest for a new hat in favour of attending his rehearsal with the Hallé Orchestra. He asked me if I could prepare Allan to play Mozart's G major Concerto K453 with the Hallé in Leeds Town Hall on 6 September. Allan's playing caused a sensation. The audience included Princess Mary, her then daughter-in-law Marion, George, and Marion's parents, Erwin and Sophie Stein. Marion said, 'This achievement should be shouted from the rooftops', because it was the first time they'd heard a prodigy since the Menuhins. And suddenly I was besieged by parents who hoped that I could turn all their children into prodigies.

A short time afterwards, I had a phone call from Ruth Railton, the founder of the National Youth Orchestra of Great Britain. She had come up to Leeds that autumn to hold auditions for the orchestra. She was also scouting for a gifted young pianist to play a concerto with the NYO at the 1954 Edinburgh Festival, and she overheard a porter talking about a young Leeds prodigy called Allan Schiller. She asked if she could hear him. So in August 1954 we went to Edinburgh, where Allan was booked to play the same Mozart concerto he had played with Sir John Barbirolli, this time with the National Youth Orchestra, conducted by Jean Martinon. The concert was on Sunday, 29 August, and it was broadcast live by the BBC. Isaac Stern was playing that year with his accompanist Alexander Zakim, and he overheard me giving Allan a lesson at eight o'clock in the morning. He came up to me and kissed me, and said, 'I'm Isaac Stern, and I have never heard teaching greater than what you are doing. No one in Europe is doing this kind of work, and if there is ever anything I can do to help, let me know. Consider me your friend.' After their concerts, the papers read, 'Isaac Stern and Allan Schiller take Edinburgh by storm.' Isaac came to Leeds the next year to play the Beethoven Violin Concerto with the Israeli Philharmonic Orchestra. One morning I got a phone call from the Queens Hotel saying that he would like to hear 'that boy' again. So I sent Geoffrey to fetch Allan, who was playing football in Roundhay Park at the time. It took him some time to locate Allan, but he played for Isaac again.

About the same time as I had started teaching Allan, I was also teaching my niece Wendy Waterman, my brother Harry's eldest child. She played Bach's D minor Concerto at the Royal Festival Hall at the age of nine. The concert was broadcast on the radio, and the BBC announcer said, 'I thought miracles were over until I saw and heard this child.' After Allan's success in Edinburgh and Wendy's in London, Ruth Railton asked if she could take both children on a tour of the Low Countries with the National Youth Orchestra in April 1955, giving concerts at the Palais des Beaux Arts in Brussels, and at the Amsterdam Concertgebouw. Wendy played the Bach D minor Concerto, and Allan played the Haydn D major. I travelled with them, and I was expected to dress the children and get them to bed. But when they were invited to a reception at the British Embassy, Ruth said that she would take the children, while I was evidently expected to stay in the background. At that point I put my foot down, and said, 'Where they are going, I'm going too.' To which she replied, 'Miss Waterman, you are keeping your pupils in a ghetto.' I was enraged. I said to her, 'For that, you will never have another pupil of mine playing with your orchestra.' She did back down later, and apologised.

Ruth could be charming, but she was absolutely ruthless. She ruled the NYO with a rod of iron. During the time that she was in charge, the boys and girls in the orchestra travelled to concerts on separate buses. Another of my pupils, a boy called Robert Bottone (who has since become Head of Music at Winchester College) once decided to sneak on to the girls' bus. He was discovered, and immediately sent home in disgrace. In spite of my disagreements with Ruth, both of my sons later joined the NYO as violinists. Robert played in the second violins in the mid-1960s while Ruth was still running the orchestra, but Paul, who played in the first violins, joined later. By then my friend Ivey Dickson had taken over, and the regime was less harsh.

However, Ruth did have both vision and determination. Her contribution to music and youth was phenomenal. I admired her for her imagination and her high musical standards, and for the opportunities that membership of the National Youth Orchestra still gives to young and brilliant musicians in this country. Of course, it did help that Ruth had a wealthy and influential husband, the newspaper magnate Cecil King. I once stayed overnight with Ruth and Cecil. Ruth was very interested in psychical research, and believed in ghosts. She told me that the bedroom where I was going to sleep was haunted. It creaked all night and I was quaking with fear, although I didn't believe in ghosts. Then in the morning, I was given a demonstration of the power of the press, which made me very nervous. At the breakfast table, Ruth said to her husband, who was eating his toast and marmalade, 'Cecil darling, Sir Robert Mayer has written a letter saying he wants some of my players because he would like to form a European orchestra, but I don't want to let him have them.' 'That little man!' said Cecil. 'He's like a beetle – I could crush him to death under my foot!' I had never heard anything like that before. Cecil King was an imposing figure, and an extremely powerful man. As chairman of the Mirror Group of newspapers, he exercised considerable influence over politicians. Apparently he believed he was born to rule. At the end of a concert Ruth once said to me, 'Cecil has to go to Number 10 now to sort out the miners' strike with Harold Wilson.' Not long afterwards I read in the papers that Cecil King had been asked to clear his desk. He had apparently been calling for the removal of the elected government of the United Kingdom. I never heard of him again.

Arthur Rubinstein once said to me about my pupils, 'They are marvellous, and you are a marvellous teacher. But, it's not how they play now, it's how they will play in twenty years' time.' When I look back now at my early so-called 'prodigy' pupils, I realise that they were not geniuses, like Mozart and Mendelssohn, they were highly gifted children. Their greatest talent at that age lay in their ability to imitate my style of playing. Allan Schiller was offered an engagement playing a Mozart concerto at the Proms when he was still only fourteen, and two more of my pupils from that period, Kathleen Jones and Nichola Gebolys, both played at the Proms when they were young teenagers. Nichola was the daughter of a Polish major in the RAF, who was based at Manchester. She played Mozart's Concerto No. 15 in B flat at the 1966 Proms with the Hallé Orchestra under John Barbirolli when she was fifteen. She later married the pianist Christian Blackshaw, but tragically died of cancer before she was forty, leaving four young children. Kathleen Jones made two appearances at the Proms, the first in 1959 when she was only fourteen, playing Mozart's D minor Concerto with the National Youth Orchestra under Walter Susskind. But her parents saw a red light – they could see the difficulties that a professional concert career would involve, and they didn't want her to put all her eggs into one basket. So Kathleen was advised to read music at university instead of to going to a conservatoire. Several of my other talented pupils chose a university education, including Paul Crossley, who went to Oxford University and then on to Paris to study with Messaien and Yvonne Loriod, and specialised in contemporary British and French piano music, and Jonathan Dunsby, who studied with me for thirteen years from the time he was eleven, throughout the time he was at Oxford University, and afterwards when he was studying for a PhD at Leeds. Jonathan won the Commonwealth Competition when he was twenty-one, and also won prizes at the Geneva and Munich competitions. He went on to hold distinguished academic appointments in London, Reading and the USA.

Another of my pupils from that early period was John Dyson. His father came from a Lithuanian Jewish family who had settled in Leeds at the turn of the twentieth century, and his Hungarian mother owned an exclusive gown shop in Leeds. John started playing the piano at an early age, encouraged by his mother. He was always passionate about music, and he came to me for piano lessons when he was a schoolboy of thirteen. I taught him for four years, and he still enjoys playing. He read classics at Oxford, and was called to the Bar in 1968. In 1993 he became a High Court Judge, and in 2010 he was appointed a Justice of the Supreme Court and Master of the Rolls, second only to the Lord Chief Justice.

Then there was Michael Roll. He was the son of a doctor who had emigrated from Vienna, and he had started playing the piano when he was four. He came to me when he was six, and gave his first recital two years later in the Leeds Art Gallery. Michael was very sensitive – I used to take him for a run in the car before he'd settle down for his lesson. At the start of a lesson he would say, 'Auntie Fanny, if you're going to make me cry, you'll make a big mistake.' And within five minutes he'd be taking out a handkerchief. He was extremely talented, although while he was at school he never intended to study music professionally, as he wanted to follow in his father's footsteps and become a doctor. Michael went to Roundhay School, and one day the headmaster called his mother to say that his piano playing was beginning to interfere with his schoolwork, especially as he was taking time off for his public performances. The matter needed to be discussed with Fanny Waterman. Mrs Roll warned the headmaster that Fanny Waterman was 'very small but very formidable', and that in any controversy, she would win. We solved the problem by inviting the headmaster and his wife to dinner, and after that Michael had no more problems at school.

In 1959, when Michael was twelve, he made his debut in the Royal Festival Hall with the National Youth Orchestra under Sir Malcolm Sargent, playing the Schumann concerto. Not long afterwards, the celebrated entertainer Victor Borge put out a message that he was looking for a young, brilliant pianist who could appear with him on his show, and perform a trick. I said, 'I think I could recommend someone' – that was Michael. He had an audition and an interview with Borge, who wanted him to begin playing the Schumann concerto (with an orchestra), and in the orchestral *tuttis*, he had to take a ham sandwich from his pocket and eat it. He did this with perfect timing, and overnight he became known as 'the Borge boy'! People were saying to him, 'You're famous now. Life is going to be all champagne receptions!' Michael's mother proudly told me that Borge was planning to take Michael on tour with him, but I said to her, 'I don't think we'll hear from Victor Borge again. Michael has stolen his thunder.' And we never did.

One by one those early prodigies all left me, some to go to different teachers. Their success just went to the parents' heads. For a long time I was simply considered 'the local piano teacher', and there came a time when other people would say to parents, 'Well, if your child is learning from a local teacher and is already playing at festivals, how much better could they become under an internationally famous teacher! They will end up playing in Carnegie Hall!' But the problem is that such-and-such a teacher might well be a famous performer, but he or she might not have the time, the energy or the commitment necessary to advance pupils' careers. It does not always follow that a famous pianist is also a great teacher. One must give one's pupils total dedication.

A case in point is Benjamin Frith, who has studied with me continuously since he was ten. He won the British National Concerto Competition when he was fourteen, and Denis Matthews described him as 'a prodigy of prodigies'. One of his triumphs was winning first prize and the Gold Medal at the 1989 Arthur Rubinstein Competition in Israel. Ben has made many highly praised recordings, and appears regularly on the BBC as a soloist and chamber musician. Even though he enjoys a busy and successful career as a concert pianist and chamber musician, he still finds time to play for me and receive my advice and help. We share the same ethos regarding piano performance.

One of the saddest aspects of my life as a teacher was the tragedy of Terence Judd. I loved Terence, who was a young and precocious pupil. On his very first visit to me, when I opened the door to him, his first words were, 'What may I call you?' I said, 'Miss Waterman', and he looked crestfallen. So I said, 'What do want to call me?' and he replied, 'Could I call you Fanny?' So I told him, 'I will give you permission to call me Fanny on condition that you never call me that if other people are around.' Terence won the National Junior Piano Playing Competition in 1967, at the age of ten, and in April 1969 he played Beethoven's First Piano Concerto in the Royal Festival Hall with the National Youth Orchestra under Hugo Rignold. His parents were both professional musicians, and his mother was a very forceful person. I remember having an argument with her when Terence was playing the Beethoven – she didn't want him rehearsing in the afternoon.

Terence was a phenomenally gifted pianist. People say he would have been one of the greatest pianists of his time, and he was certainly one of my most gifted pupils. At only seventeen years of age he was placed fourth in the 1979 Tchaikovsky Competition. I shall never forget hearing the terrible news on the radio not long afterwards that a brilliant young pianist's body had been discovered at the foot of Beachy Head. He was only twenty-two years old.

Not everybody is able to cope with the rigours of life as a concert pianist. It requires huge reserves of physical and emotional stamina to cope with the relentless pressure. I still find it inexplicable as to why some young pianists flourish while others disappear without trace. Is it personality? Strength of character? No one knows how they will cope with the ravages of life – they have to learn to deal with bad notices and live with disappointment. They will fall in love, get married, maybe go through the trauma of divorce. It's not just playing the piano, it's the whole package. In the end, it comes down to survival.

6

MARION

It was through my growing reputation as a teacher that I came into contact with the dearest friend of my lifetime. As time went on, Geoffrey and I began to move in different social circles. I became very friendly with Lady Dorothy Parkinson, the daughter of Baron Bingley of Bramham Park, and the niece of Lord Halifax, the last Viceroy of India and Foreign Secretary in the Chamberlain government at the outbreak of war. Dorothy was an enthusiastic violinist, and owned a Stradivarius violin. I used to go to her beautiful house outside Harrogate to play chamber music. Dorothy moved in very wide social circles – royalty, military, business, and so forth. If she had a party, Geoffrey and I were always invited, and although we came from a very different social background, it never made any difference. Dorothy was truly classless, and music was our bond.

One day she rang me up to say, 'I've got Princess Mary and her daughter-in-law coming over for tea. Would you like to come and bring some of your pupils?' And that was my first introduction to Marion, Countess of Harewood.

Marion had been born in Vienna. Her father, Erwin Stein, was a distinguished musicologist who had studied with Schoenberg, and had begun his career as an opera conductor. Erwin Stein came from a Jewish family, although he had converted to Protestantism. In 1920, while conducting in Darmstadt, Erwin had met Sophie Bachmann, the widowed daughter of a German Lutheran pastor. Sophie, who had a son and two stepsons from her first marriage, was making ends meet by taking in lodgers, including Erwin Stein.

After their marriage they lived in Vienna, where Erwin worked as artistic adviser to Universal Edition, then the major European publisher of contemporary music. Their only child, named Maria Donata Nannetta Paulina Gustava Erwina Wilhelmina, but known as Marion, was born on 18 October 1926. She inherited her mother's beauty and elegance, and her father's passion for music, especially the music of Mahler, of which Erwin Stein was a great champion. Marion began to learn the piano as a child, and she and her father used to play through piano duet reductions of symphonic scores.

But in 1938 Erwin Stein, being Jewish, was forced to leave Vienna when Austria was annexed by Nazi Germany. He was offered a job as music editor by the London-based firm of Boosey & Hawkes, the British agent of Universal Edition, and the family left Vienna in September 1938 – Erwin first, followed a few days later by Sophie and the thirteen-year-old Marion. They had to leave all their possessions behind, including Erwin's library of scores, but they later found out that they had escaped just in time to avoid being arrested. Marion's older half-brother stayed in Germany and joined the Luftwaffe. He was killed in action during the war.

Like many Jewish refugees, Erwin Stein was interned during the early months of the war on the Isle of Man, where his fellow internees included members of the soon-to-be-formed Amadeus Quartet. After his release the family settled down to life in wartime London, at the same time that I was studying at the Royal College of Music. They lived in a flat in Kensington, and Marion won a scholarship to Kensington High School. During the Blitz her school was bombed in the same air raid that destroyed the Queen's Hall, and for a while the girls were evacuated to Oxford, just as I was. She continued her piano studies, and on leaving school she went to the Royal College of Music to study under Kendall Taylor. I don't think she ever really intended to become a professional concert pianist: she spent only two terms at the College, and then studied for a while in Brussels, as well as privately with Franz Osborn, but her true mentor was Clifford Curzon.

Through her father's work at Boosey & Hawkes, Marion came into contact with Benjamin Britten, who at that time was a young and rising composer. Erwin Stein had met Britten when the composer and his mother visited Vienna in the autumn of 1934, and the Steins now became close friends of Britten and his partner, Peter Pears. Sophie became a housekeeper for Britten and Pears, and in 1944, after a fire at their flat, the family moved into Britten's maisonette in St John's Wood. Marion, who was by now a very beautiful young woman, was living there while Britten was finishing *Peter Grimes* and beginning work on *The Rape of Lucretia*. According to Britten's librettist Ronald Duncan, she inspired the lullaby 'She sleeps as a rose upon the night' from *Lucretia*. As a pianist, Marion was so overawed by Britten's superior skill in that direction, that she couldn't bring herself to practise while he was in the flat. She felt so intimidated that Clifford Curzon had to find her a practice studio elsewhere. But she didn't only admire Britten as a musician. It wasn't long before she fell in love with him, but although he was devoted to her, his sexual interests clearly lay elsewhere.

It was through Britten that Marion met her first husband. In June 1948 she and her parents attended the first Festival that Britten and Pears had founded in the small Suffolk fishing village of Aldeburgh. The Festival's president was George Lascelles, the Earl of Harewood. George, who was the same age as my husband Geoffrey, was King George V's eldest grandchild. His mother, Princess Mary, had married Viscount Lascelles, heir to an earldom whose family seat was at Harewood House, near Harrogate. George had served as an officer in the Grenadier Guards during the war. He was wounded and captured in Italy by the Germans, and had spent some time imprisoned in Colditz. In March 1945 Hitler signed his death warrant, but the SS general in charge of Colditz refused to carry out the order and released him instead.

George became the 7th Earl at the age of only twenty-four, after his father's death in May 1947. From childhood he had been a passionate music-lover, which was – and still is – unusual for a British aristocrat. His uncle, the Prince of Wales, later the Duke of Windsor, once said, 'It's very odd about George and music. His parents were quite normal you know – liked horses and dogs and the country.' George had spent his time as a POW studying *Grove's Dictionary of Music* – he said he got as far as the letter T before he was released. But his main enthusiasm was opera, and after the war he joined the staff of the Royal Opera House. He later edited *Kobbé's Opera Book* for thirty years, and in the 1970s he became managing director of English National Opera. In the late 1940s he had seemed an obvious choice to be the president of a new music festival whose founder was shaping up to become the finest English opera composer for over two hundred years.

George was introduced to the Steins at a party after the Festival. He had the greatest respect for Erwin, and he was bowled over by Marion's beauty. Before long he had asked her to marry him, but because he was a member of the Royal Family, and in the royal line of succession, King George VI had to give his permission. Marion was duly presented at court, and although George's grandmother Queen Mary had reservations about the prospective bride, saying, 'She's Jewish, and she doesn't hunt', the couple was given permission to marry. On 29 September 1949, shortly before her twenty-third birthday, the Viennese refugee Marion Stein left her parents' flat in Kensington to become the Countess of Harewood. The wedding at St Mark's Church, North Audley Street, was attended by every member of the Royal Family, and the reception was held at St James's Palace. Britten wrote a wedding cantata for the bridal couple, *Amo ergo sum*, which was performed during the service by Joan Cross and Peter Pears.

Although Marion had given a few public concerts, and in the summer before her marriage had played the piano in performances of *The Little Sweep* and the cantata *St Nicolas* at the Aldeburgh Festival, piano playing now took second place to her duties as *châtelaine* of a magnificent Palladian mansion packed with Chippendale furniture and priceless art treasures, with an interior designed by Robert Adam, and a park by Capability Brown. Her introduction to aristocratic life at Harewood can't have been particularly easy, as both she and George were very young, and

George's regal mother, Princess Mary, remained in residence, rather than moving to a dower house as was normally the custom in such families. But Princess Mary became very fond of her daughter-in-law, and Marion soon adjusted to Yorkshire life. She and George divided their time between Yorkshire and London, where they bought a house in Orme Square in Bayswater, and George became artistic director of the Edinburgh and Leeds Festivals. Their first son, David, was born in 1950, followed by James in 1953 and Jeremy two years later. It looked like a perfect partnership, with George and Marion united by their love of music. George was very generous to Marion's parents, and supported Sophie after Erwin died in 1958.

Shortly after I had first met Marion at Lady Parkinson's house, I had a letter from her asking me if I would take her eldest son David as a pupil. He was about eight years old, and at prep school. I still have Marion's letter saying, 'My husband and I would very much like it if you would teach our son David in the holidays, which we spend at Harewood.' I always insisted that a parent should attend the lessons of their young children, even if they themselves didn't know anything about music, and Marion was very happy to come with David. Unfortunately he hadn't inherited his parents' talent or love for music – I remember saying to him, 'David, I could never make a pianist out of you, because you never practise!'

When I first began to teach David, and to really get to know Marion, I was very cautious about what I said to her. Although her life, like mine, had started out very differently, I remembered that she was now a member of the Royal Family, and I was still only at the beginning of my career. When I was buying my blouses at C & A, she was going to Paris with her mother-in-law, Princess Mary, to shop at Worth. When my children were very young and we were visiting Marion at Harewood, they were bemused by the fact that you could go through a door and find yourself in a splendid room with members of the public walking through it, while the family lived behind doors marked 'Private' – the distinction between public and private seemed rather confused! But although Marion's married life started as a glamorous fairytale, it ended miserably, while Geoffrey and I remained idyllically happy.

By the early 1960s Marion's marriage was under strain. While waiting to board a flight at Milan Airport on one of his many trips abroad, George had met Patricia Tuckwell, an Australian violinist and former model. Geoffrey and I were aware of the rumours which began to fly around Leeds of troubles in the Harewood marriage, but at first I refused to believe them. Marion was not given to gossiping or self-pity – she was very reserved about her private life. On one of the few occasions when she confided in me, I asked her if she had smelt danger when Patricia was included in their parties at Harewood. To which she replied, 'Yes, but what could I do about it?' She tried so hard to keep her marriage together. I remember once sitting with Marion's mother, overlooking the lake at Harewood. It was the late summer of 1964, and an extremely difficult time for everybody. George had just had a son with Patricia, and was putting pressure on Marion to give him a divorce. The Queen and the Duke of Edinburgh were due to open the new Forth Road Bridge and to attend the last weekend of the Edinburgh Festival, where George was the artistic director. Marion had told the Royal Household that she would not be at George's side, but in the end, to avoid further gossip, she relented. Reflecting on the tragedy of her daughter's marriage, Sophie sighed and confided to me, 'It would have been better if Marion had been married to a cobbler.'

The year 1965 was dreadful for Marion. She and George finally separated and she was obliged to leave Harewood House. She also lost both her own mother and her mother-in-law, Princess Mary, who died of a heart attack while out walking in the park. The Harewoods' separation was particularly traumatic, and Marion sometimes took refuge with us to escape the intrusive attentions of the press. We shielded her from them – reporters were even camped on my doorstep at one point. Two years later George and Marion were finally divorced, much to royal disapproval – it was the first royal divorce, and attracted much unwelcome publicity. Marion was awarded custody of the children and the house in

Orme Square, while George was cut out from royal circles for ten years. He was not invited to the funeral of his uncle, the Duke of Windsor, nor to Princess Anne's wedding.

He was also cast out from Ben's and Peter's court, and resigned as director of the Aldeburgh Festival. Ben and Peter had supported Marion loyally throughout all her traumas and distress, and she remained very close to them. Geoffrey and I sometimes stayed at Curlews, her house at Thorpeness near Aldeburgh. I remember being there when Rostropovich was playing at the Festival. We had some marvellous times. We went down to the beach early in the morning to get some lovely lobster from a fisherman called Billy. I used to cook occasionally for Ben and Peter, although I once remember cooking some meat for them which I left too long in the oven – it turned out like leather! Those times went on until Marion sold Curlews and lived only at Orme Square. That house became a magnet for the greatest international musical personalities of our time – people like Giulini, Maria Callas, Ben and Peter, Tito Gobbi, and especially Mstislav Rostropovich, who had met Marion at Aldeburgh. As soon as he arrived, there would be screams of delight in the hall and bear-hugs all round. Marion was so glamorous – she lit up a room, and everyone wanted to meet her. You felt privileged to be at the court of Marion, Countess of Harewood.

Marion was closely involved in the first four Leeds competitions, and remained joint chairman with me until she resigned in 1983. She and I also created our series of piano tutors, the *Waterman–Harewood Piano Method*. After Ben died in 1976 she became a trustee of the Britten–Pears Foundation, set up to oversee and fund a variety of activities connected with Britten's works, including performances, recordings and publications. I was very pleased when in 2008 she was deservedly awarded a CBE for her services to music. She had never shown any jealousy at all when I received my honours – she was genuinely pleased that my achievements had been officially recognised, and held a party in my honour after I was awarded the DBE in 2005. After Murray Perahia's great success at the 1972 Leeds Competition, she invited him to Aldeburgh, and introduced him to Ben and Peter. As a result, Murray became an artistic director of the Festival, planning and performing many concerts both as soloist and chamber music player, and maintaining its best traditions.

Marion's eldest son, David, had a successful career as a television producer before he succeeded to the earldom in 2011 after his father died. Towards the end of her life Marion was interviewed by the BBC, and was asked what she regarded as her greatest achievement. Without any hesitation she said it was helping to found the Leeds International Piano Competition.

Interlude I
A Tale of Two Dogs

Marion had a dog called Whizzy, and I decided that we should have a dog too. Geoffrey had always liked dogs: we have kept a school essay he wrote when he was eight, called 'An Imaginary Letter from My Pet'. It reads:

My Dear Master

I am writing to thank you for many things, and also to bring to your notice a few complaints.

First of all I have to thank you for that lovely birthday present you gave me, that comfortable, roomy, and altogether desirable kennel. Now, for one of the complaints, will you tell cook not to give me any more soft chicken bones, because yesterday she gave me one and said it was a terribly hard bone, so I gave a hard snap and bit it clean in two and cracked my tooth. You may laugh, but take it from me it's no laughing matter because it hurt.

Now do you think you could do me a favour? Just ask your mother if I could have a little room at the end of the garden in which to bury my bones. By the way, are you friendly with the man next door? If not you might tell him this from me that I don't want him throwing flowerpots at me. But I must say goodbye because I can smell my dinner at the door of my kennel. But all the same

I remain
Your faithful and trusty pet
SANDY

Although he liked the idea of having a dog, Geoffrey thought we were too busy and that we weren't psychologically ready. But the children were keen, and we acquired a long-haired dachshund called Rip. Inevitably, Geoffrey, rather than the children, ended up doing most of the work of looking after him. In the beginning, when Rip was a puppy, he was making a mess all over the house. Our friend Lady Stevens, wife of the Vice-Chancellor of Leeds University, told us, 'If he makes a mess, get a piece of paper, roll it up, and tap his tail!' But it didn't seem to work. Eventually I said to Geoffrey and the boys, 'This dog must go.' On the morning that Rip was meant to be taken away, we couldn't find him. We went up and down the road, asking people if they had seen a long-haired dachshund. He finally turned up two days later, and from then on he never left my side. If the doorbell rang, he would shake himself from a deep sleep and follow me to the door to see who was there. He sat under the piano, listening while I gave lessons, and when Paul was little he used to sit under it with him. Rip acquired an excellent knowledge of all the Beethoven sonatas! And we had to learn to live with a neurotic dog.

Rip was very naughty. I was once preparing a dinner party for twenty-two people. I had made a starter of chopped liver, which was laid out on the table. Just as our guests were arriving, Geoffrey went into the dining room, and then came into the kitchen, asking, 'Have you put the starter out?' I said, 'Yes, it's already on the table.' 'No it isn't,' he replied. I went to look, and there were twenty-two perfectly clean side plates. We were utterly mystified as to where the liver had vanished, until Geoffrey noticed that several of the wine glasses were lying on their sides in a neat row down the centre of the table. We deduced that Rip, whose legs were extremely short, must somehow have jumped up on to the table and devoured the liver, while walking along wagging his long tail as he made his triumphant progress from one end to the other. Fortunately, I had some smoked salmon in the fridge, so the supper was saved.

Marion's Jack Russell terrier Whizzy was just as bad. He was the bane of her life. She used to give grand parties at her house in

Orme Square, and I remember one particular time when Giulini and Annie Fischer had been giving a concert and afterwards came round to Orme Square to dinner. When we got up together to get the food for the second course, we were full of consternation. Marion came up to me and pointed at the floor. I saw that Whizzy had performed under the table, and she whispered, 'Shall I bring a brush and pan?' I said, 'No, let's take a risk on no one noticing', even though the 'evidence' was only an inch from Giulini's beautiful patent-leather shoes. So Marion pushed it under the curtain with her foot.

Whizzy was a nightmare. He used to perform up against the curtains in Orme Square, and they faded badly. He even cocked a leg up against another man's dog while we were out for a walk. The owner was very cross, remarking, 'It's about time you got this dog trained!' We felt very embarrassed. We weren't really dog lovers, but we spent a great deal of time discussing the relative misbehaviours of both our pets.

Eventually Whizzy was taken up to Harewood, which was a more suitable environment for him than London. When Marion was still living there, I occasionally used to have lunch with her and her mother-in-law, Princess Mary. I remember once being at a small luncheon party when a terrible odour began to pervade the atmosphere. We all looked at each other, feeling guilty. Who was the culprit? Princess Mary took her napkin and wafted it around to get rid of the smell. Then we noticed Whizzy, who was hiding under the table. We were all relieved to be exonerated!

Rip lived to the great age of nineteen. Eventually there came a point where he couldn't really get up any more, and people started falling over him. We summoned the vet, who examined him, and told us that he was by now a very unhappy dog, and we should consider having him put down. I was sitting in the kitchen, and Rip was lifted on my lap, shivering. I remembered that Ben Britten – a great dog lover – held his dog when he had his final injection, and I thought that I must be as brave. So I held Rip as his life ebbed away. He kept his eyes fixed on me all the time. It was awful. That was at ten o'clock in the morning. Then on the BBC's one o'clock news on the same day came the announcement that a young British pianist had taken a one-way ticket to the South Coast and drowned himself. It was my pupil Terence Judd. That was a terrible day.

7

THOUGHTS ON TEACHING

Study is unending.
ROBERT SCHUMANN

The fullest possible understanding between teacher and pupil is
one of the most important conditions for fruitful teaching.
HEINRICH NEUHAUS

Teaching is a great profession, but a great teacher doesn't overteach. Instead he or she should guide and teach a pupil to think independently.

If you want to be able to play the piano well, you must start young, with an excellent teacher. That teacher must have very fine ears, but unfortunately those ears cannot simply be passed on to the pupil. And that is one of the biggest challenges. The ability to hear, listen, and assess how to improve a performance whilst respecting and staying true to the composer is the most priceless gift that a teacher can impart to a performing artist.

How do I choose my beginner pupils? I reply that I don't choose the pupils, I choose the parents. The great piano pedagogue Heinrich Neuhaus, whose pupils included Sviatoslav Richter, Emil Gilels and Radu Lupu, wrote that eventually one comes to realise 'how important it is for a good pianist to have supportive parents ... One cannot create talent but one can recognise it from the outset and create the culture, which is the soil on which that talent prospers and flourishes.' I always encourage a parent to be present at lessons of the young child. Even if they don't know anything about music themselves, they can supervise practice at home and help the child to progress between lessons. It's amazing how they begin to hear the difference in sound.

I do beware of giving parents false hopes that their son or daughter might become a concert pianist, as I know only too well the difficulty of that very lonely career. So when a parent comes to me asking if I will teach their child, I say to them from the start, 'Right, let's treat this as an experiment. If I enjoy teaching your child, and they enjoy their lessons, that will be all well and good. They may not end up playing professionally, but in any case, being able to play an instrument is a marvellous discipline which will give your child pleasure and enjoyment to the end of their life, and can open up the gates of the world.'

I start by teaching my young pupils the geography of the piano. Finding all the Cs on the keyboard, for instance, can be like a game. But once they start putting notes together, I get them to think about gradations of tone right from the start, and particularly tonal colour, even when playing scales. Encouragement should be part of every lesson, and marks should be awarded for the week's good work. I had a very young Chinese pupil, just five years old, and when I asked him about the mark he had been given, which was disappointing, he turned to me and said, 'Well, it's only a matter of opinion!'

At the first lesson, I give my young pupils a list of Ten Musical Commandments.

- Keep your back straight and your fingers rounded.
- Practise regularly every day.
- Before you start playing any unfamiliar music, clap the rhythm, counting the beats aloud.
- With your teacher's help, choose fingering most suited to your hand, write it on the music in pencil and change it only when absolutely necessary.
- Hands separately before hands together.
- Practise slowly, and begin to build up speed only when you feel secure.

- When practising and repeating phrases, give yourself 'listening time'. Correct any mistake on the spot and play the phrase slowly several times before going on. Never put your foot on the accelerator until your teacher gives you permission to speed up.
- Clap the rhythmic patterns of a piece through before you start playing it.
- Follow all the composer's dynamic markings, making the difference between the six levels from *pp* to *ff*.
- Listen to every note you play on the piano, and strive for the most beautiful sound.

The teacher should observe the pupil's body movement, making sure that he or she doesn't swing or cross his or her legs, and that the shoulders are relaxed. I say to my young pupils, 'What parts of the body do you use to play?' They answer, 'Fingers, wrists, arms, upper arms, shoulders', and some of them remember to say, 'and your legs, if you are pedalling'. And then I will say, 'And what about your heart? You have to remember to play with feeling.' Even small children must think about the soul of the music they're playing, it's not just the notes. 'And what about your ears? What about your eyes? What about your brain? You are like a musical computer.'

Technique starts with tone production. I developed an idea of how I could help my small pupils to make the piano sing, which is the first point of departure. I say, 'I'll show you a game. This phrase is like an umbrella, think of the notes going round the curve of the edge and each one has a different tonal value.'

There are very few pupils who can produce what I want, that rhythmic vitality, the structure of the piece, how to communicate with your audience, the tonal colours. The sheer tonal range in between *pianissimo* and *forte* is truly amazing. Even on a single note we can play from the softest to the loudest sound – we can produce a large tone without harshness, or a *pianissimo* that will carry to the back of the gallery. I like to compare this tonal variety to an artist's palette – just as there are many different shades of blue, from the palest powder blue to the deepest Pacific blue, so there are many different nuances of piano tone. I agree with Neuhaus: 'If a player doesn't give enough thought to the extraordinary dynamic wealth and diversity of tone which the piano can provide, but concentrates mainly on technique, he is incapable of listening to himself. The resulting musical web is as drab as army khaki.'

The first element of tone production requires that pianists learn how to listen to the quality of every sound they produce. Then comes the question of touch, which all depends on the speed of the key descent. By controlling the speed at which the piano key descends to the key bed, you control both the volume and the tonal quality. To make the point to my younger pupils, I ask them to imagine that they have a rubber ball in their hand. If they let it slip gently to the ground, it will produce less sound than if it were bounced vigorously. Tone quality is also affected by the position of the fingers, which vary according to whether you are playing brilliant passage-work, when the fingers should be bent, or passages needing a fuller tone, which require flatter fingers. And the other essential component of fine tone-production is a flexible wrist and a relaxed arm. There must be no tension anywhere, especially in the shoulders.

The second aspect of training is learning to become a fine musician. You can't divorce technique from musicianship. The great composers have left us only their manuscripts. We need to bring those notes to life. We are often given not only the notes, but also some clues as to how to play them, and a pianist needs to be a musical detective, able to deduce the composer's intentions from such indications as the title, tempo markings, key signatures, dynamics, phrase marks, accents and silences. Silences and pauses are almost more important than the notes and intensify the music. The great pianist Artur Schnabel said, 'The notes I handle no better than many pianists. But the pauses between the notes – ah, that is where the art resides.' The student must learn how important it is to follow and memorise the composer's markings, for to ignore them is a musical crime.

A fine teacher will guide pupils to acquire knowledge of the repertoire of the great composers, many of whom have written beautiful miniature pieces especially for young performers. When a great composer is creating music, he is feeling the same emotions as we do. So I say to my young pupils, 'Do you always feel happy, or do you always feel sad? When you're playing, I want you to tell me how you think the composer felt while he was writing this piece – it's no use playing a funeral march as if it's a walk in the park. Think about Beethoven composing his wonderful music – he couldn't hear it, because he was deaf, and was suffering from cancer of the stomach. He was lonely and neglected, and yet he produced these great works of art. And the least you can do, however young you are, is to use those markings, because you've got to creep into the soul of the composer.' I ask children to tell me as many different moods as they can express, and even at age ten or eleven, they come up with a whole series: 'angry', 'looking forward', 'excited', and so on. They should imagine that they are actors in a play. This big black block of wood can be magically transformed into an orchestra, a singer, a string quartet. It can imitate the souls of other instruments. Anton Rubinstein said about the piano, 'You think it is one instrument? It is a hundred instruments!' The pupil must learn how to communicate from the start, and to make the listener listen.

When I am teaching more advanced students and budding concert artists, I encourage them to think *orchestrally* – I tell them that sonatas are like symphonies for the piano. The piano texture in a low register might resemble the tone of a double-bass or cello, the middle register can sound like a viola, and the high register like a violin. And the melodic line in several of the slow move- ments from Mozart's piano concertos sounds like an operatic aria. You have to remember, for instance, that Beethoven or Mozart loved the viola, and to bring out that middle voice on the piano, you must have the ability to play polyphonically with several strands, with independence of fingers. With the voicing of two or three notes, it's the balance of the fingers, and what you are aiming for is the blending of the notes, with the addition of the pedal. The sustaining pedal, as Chopin said, is the soul of the piano. It doesn't just prolong the sound of a note or chord, it also enriches the sound by adding an aura of vibrations and harmonies, and allows the player to colour the tone. I tell my pupils to listen for the vibrations when they finish a phrase with the pedal down. That is so beautiful on the piano, it produces an ethereal chord. It's not the first impact of that sound, it's something that happens the mini-second after that, and that's the most beautiful effect. And you're dealing in micro-seconds. You can go on infinitely dissecting a phrase, and yet, when you put it together, it's all in the voicing. The passagework in a Chopin nocturne, for instance, should be as gossamer-delicate as a butterfly's wing.

To play a simple melody with fine tone and rhythm is one of the greatest pianistic challenges. Sometimes you can struggle with a beautiful piece of Schumann, for instance, that is technically quite simple. If you're not careful, you will overplay it. It's the *second* simplicity that is so beautiful. When I am listening to a child playing an easy Mozart piece, I say that the simplicity of that play-ing is quite different from the second simplicity of a great artist who has striven to invest the piece with all his or her emotions, not synthetically, but with vision and integrity. That can take a life-time. When you think of the opening of Beethoven's Fourth Piano Concerto, how pianists at all stages have struggled with that opening chord, to get the top note singing, and all the others just melting. It's like considering a great actor performing Hamlet's famous speech 'To be, or not to be, that is the question'. Those words can be spoken in so many different ways, with such variety of emphasis and inflection, and can mean something quite different every time. There are so many inflections in *staccato*, for instance: some notes marked *staccato* can be quite long, others very short, like string *pizzicati. Rubato* is practically impossible to teach. One needs to listen to a great singer, such as Dame Janet Baker, as the intake of breath, the respiration, is so important.

Personal energy is crucial to my own teaching, and is vital to the pupil's improvement. A teacher's responsibility is to ensure a continuous flow of energy level from teacher to pupil. I teach as if any of my pupils might become a concert pianist. There's no way I can say, 'Well, I'll just sit back and let them play through this.' As soon as I hear some room for improvement, I sit at the keyboard and ask them to imitate what I am trying to do. It is vitally important for a teacher to keep playing him- or herself.

During a lesson, I follow the score and make notes and comments. At the end of the student's performance I will always find something to praise, and make general critical comments. Then we begin to work together on every note, bar or phrase in the greatest detail. Just the opening phrase of a piece could take up a whole lesson – the first chord of Beethoven's Fourth Piano Concerto, for instance, or the relationship between sound and silence in the first bars of Liszt's B minor Sonata. Nonetheless, I always encourage my students to bear in mind the rhythmic architecture of a piece – to think in paragraphs, not short phrases. We are partners in a process of exploration and discovery, until the student has clarified his or her own interpretation. I comment on details, and besides playing myself, I will also, depending on the student's age and level of attainment, demonstrate by singing, conducting and (if they are very young), making up words to fit the music, capturing its mood by quoting from a poem, even making them dance! This process is continuous throughout the lesson. I always give credit for anything my pupils have picked up by listening for themselves.

I have long chats with my pupils. Respect and understanding between teacher and pupil evolves over time. But I tell them that ultimately they must take the final responsibility for their per- formance. They must remember that it will not be how I wanted them to play, it's what *they* feel about the music. At that point, the umbilical cord that connects teacher and pupil is finally cut.

Some things can't be taught. You can't teach charm, or teach passion, or teach humour. If you listen to Brendel playing a Haydn sonata, he emphasizes the lightness and humour through his playing – and the audience will respond with smiles or even laughs.

There are so many things a teacher can't do, but you can inspire, demonstrate, and love. I always say to my pupils, 'Keep in touch with your teachers and remember that learning is forever and there is no age at which you can stop, even at ninety-five!'

8

A DREAM COMES TRUE

By 1961 my teaching career was well established. In my musical life I spent hours thinking about how I could inspire a young child to become a great pianist. I would give lessons to anyone whom I thought had exceptional talent, and hoped that the young pupils would develop into great artists. Five of my highly gifted pupils performed concertos with great conductors and orchestras of the day before they were twelve years old. But they all left me in turn because I was referred to as 'the local piano teacher', an appellation which I secretly resented. So after they began to leave, I thought, 'Why don't I do for the rest of the pianistic world what I have achieved in Leeds?' I had produced these wonderful pianists, and also helped to get their future careers going.

Before I fall asleep, there's a moment when I am neither awake nor asleep. And it's in those moments that I suddenly get a flash of inspiration. That was how the competition came into being.

In 1961 I woke Geoffrey up with an idea that I wished to organise an international piano competition. He responded, 'It won't work here in Leeds. You need the resources of a capital city.' Looked at in the cold light of day, Geoffrey had a point. Why had London never thought of hosting a competition, with the resources available from no less than four music conservatoires, as well as recital venues such as the Wigmore Hall, and a major international concert hall in the Royal Festival Hall? Leeds didn't even have a resident orchestra. It had the grand high Victorian Town Hall, where celebrities such as Rubinstein and Schnabel and wonderful choirs had performed. It also had the experience of the

Leeds Triennial Festival, but this had unfortunately gone through a difficult period in the 1950s and had almost foundered on financial rocks.

In the early 1960s there were few international piano competitions. The oldest, the International Chopin Competition, had started up in Warsaw in 1927. It had been held just five times since, most recently in 1960 when Maurizio Pollini was the winner. There were two others that were well established. The Queen Elisabeth of the Belgians competition in Brussels had produced some distinguished winners – Emil Gilels was the first pianist to win in 1938, with Moura Lympany coming second and Jakob Flier third; and they were followed in the 1950s by first prize-winners Leon Fleisher and Vladimir Ashkenazy. The first Geneva Competition was won by Arturo Benedetti Michelangeli in 1939, and its subsequent winners had included some fine pianists – Friedrich Gulda, Maria Tipo, and Martha Argerich in 1957, the same year as she also won the Busoni Competition in Bolzano, Italy. Others were much more recent – the Enescu Competition in Bucharest, hidden away behind the Iron Curtain, and the International Tchaikovsky Competition in Moscow. The first pianist to win that competition, in 1958, was the American Van Cliburn. His sensational success, beating the Russian competition at their own game by playing concertos by Tchaikovsky and Rachmaninov, inspired a group of enthusiastic and wealthy fans to found the first American piano competition, named after Van Cliburn. That competition was one of the very few not based in a capital city. The United Kingdom had never had a competition like these, yet five years later we were setting up the Leeds.

The morning after my flash of inspiration I rang Marion, the Countess of Harewood, whose son David I was teaching the piano. She was enthusiastic about the idea: without a moment's hesitation she said, 'Let's try.' We realised that in order to make it work we needed solid finance, local support and an international presence, in order to attract a top-class jury. Marion's social connections as Countess of Harewood, both at home and abroad, coupled with my own reputation as a musician, were very

Princess Mary, the competition's first Patron

Marion and I

With my dog, Rip

Lady Dorothy Parkinson

Geoffrey acting as the platform announcer

The jury for the 1966 competition, with Nadia Boulanger in the centre

Competitors at the 1966 competition, with Marion and myself

With Lord Boyle, Chairman of the jury

Nadia Boulanger on the jury

Murray Perahia

Four Leeds winners: Rafael Orozco, Murray Perahia, Michael Roll, Radu Lupu

Backstage with Rostropovich, Jeremy Thorpe
and Perahia

With Sir Edward Heath, at the piano
at my home

Family photo with grandchildren Carmella, Gemma and Alexandra,
and Paul, Robert and Geoffrey behind us

important in getting the competition off the ground, but the first major offer of help actually came from a member of Leeds's close-knit Jewish community. A wealthy local businessman, Jack Lyons, agreed to donate £1000 to start up the competition, which we estimated would cost about £8000 in total. Jack Lyons had been born in Leeds, the son of a Polish Jewish immigrant who worked in the clothing trade. His was a real rags-to-riches story – Jack went to the USA to study at Columbia University and then on to Canada where he met his wife, a singer called Roslyn Rosenbaum. After he came back to England, he and his brother built up a huge clothing retail empire which by the 1960s was one of the largest in the whole country. He used some of his substantial personal fortune for philanthropic purposes – he endowed a new concert hall at York University, and a theatre at the Royal Academy of Music, and gave generously to hospitals and universities. We were very pleased to have his offer of financial support.

We also approached Leeds City Council to help us with funding. The council was Labour-controlled, and half of the councillors thought that the event would be too 'elitist', while the others didn't like the idea of private patronage and thought it should be wholly council-funded. So at first they rejected the motion, but then Jack Lyons threatened to withdraw his support, and after a huge row, the council finally agreed to match Jack's donation. We also had offers of support from the Leeds Festival, and from the Arts Council of Great Britain. Two more local businessmen – Charles Tapp, the owner of a large local printing firm, and Norman Wilkinson – jointly donated the second-prize money of £500; Granada Television Network offered a third prize of £250; and other local businesses, banks and private individuals gave a further 15 prizes of £50 each for the second-stage runners-up. The rest came from some tireless fund-raising through concerts and coffee mornings, together with the money we anticipated would come from box-office takings on Finals Night, when the finalists would play a concerto in Leeds Town Hall with the Royal Liverpool Philharmonic Orchestra conducted by John Pritchard.

Apart from Marion, myself and Jack Lyons, the other members of the original committee included Geoffrey, Roslyn Lyons, three Leeds city councillors, George Harewood, the Vicar of Leeds, Lady Parkinson, the headmaster of Leeds Grammar School Charles Woodford, Charles Tapp, and Professor James Denny, from the Music Department at the University of Leeds. He also sat on the executive committee, chaired by Marion, whose members included our treasurer, Cecil Mazey (a retired regional bank manager); Maurice Hare, a master at Leeds Grammar School; myself, and my childhood friend Joan Valentine, whose help with the competition over many years was to prove invaluable. Marion's mother-in-law, Princess Mary, who at that time was Chancellor of the University of Leeds, agreed to be the competition's Patron, and to present the prizes, including the winner's Princess Mary Gold Medal. The Lord Mayor of Leeds was the competition's first President, with the Vicar of Leeds and the Vice-Chancellor of the University, Sir Charles Morris, as Vice-Presidents.

I was a very good friend of the university's Vice-Chancellor Elect, Sir Roger Stevens, a former diplomat who had been the British ambassador to Persia, and his wife Constance, who was a fine amateur pianist with whom I played every Thursday morning. We realised from the start that we would need the university's help. One of the problems we had in Leeds was the lack of facilities for practice and accommodation, not to mention a first-class recital hall. The University solved both problems by offering the use of one of its student halls of residence, Tetley Hall, to feed and house the competitors with the help of an efficient army of volunteer helpers, and also its light and airy Great Hall, which had a good quality concert grand piano, for the earlier rounds. The residents of Leeds responded magnificently to our appeal for families possessing pianos of a good enough standard who would be willing to allow young people – many of whom would speak little or no English – into their homes to practise up to six hours a day. Amazingly, we got around eighty positive responses.

The first competition would be held in mid-September 1963, and we sent brochures to music colleges and conservatories in the

UK and around the world, inviting applications from young pianists, aged under thirty. We decided at the start that what we would be looking for would be musicianship and beauty of tone, rather than flashy virtuosity. Marion and I selected the repertoire, concentrating on the music we both loved. The repertoire for the first of the three stages offered a choice of one work from each of a limited selection of classics – Bach's *Italian Concerto* or his E flat Prelude and Fugue; four études by Chopin, and three Beethoven sonatas (including the *Appassionata*). Twenty competitors would then go through to the second stage, in which candidates were invited to compile a short recital programme drawn from each of four categories. The first contained substantial works by Mozart, Beethoven, Chopin, Schumann and Brahms; the second, virtuoso pieces by Liszt, Debussy, Ravel and Albéniz; the third, works by four twentieth-century composers, Bartók, Prokofiev, Stravinsky and Schoenberg.

It was Marion's idea that every competitor should have to play a slow piece, so we commissioned a compulsory test piece from her great friend, Benjamin Britten, who said he would be happy to write a piece in honour of the competition. *Notturno*, which reflects Britten's preoccupation at that time with the mood and imagery of night, turned out to be his last solo piano work. Marion and I both believed that this delicate, atmospheric and subtle piece, which is particularly designed to showcase musicianship and imagination rather than virtuosity, would sort out the musicians from the mere technicians, and would encapsulate the spirit of the new Leeds Competition. It still remains part of the competition's repertoire fifty years later.

Thanks to both of our contacts, we assembled an impressive list of international names for our first jury. Its chairman was to be Sir Arthur Bliss, Master of the Queen's Music. The other British members were the conductor John Pritchard, Marion's former mentor Clifford Curzon, and the distinguished musicologist, critic and broadcaster, Hans Keller. Like Marion, Hans had come to England as a refugee from pre-war Vienna, and like George Harewood, he was also a fanatical football supporter. In early 1963

Marion visited the Soviet Union with Britten, and as a result of her discussions at the Soviet Ministry of Culture, the great pianist and teacher Jakob Flier, a specialist in the Romantic repertoire and a veteran of international competitions, was allowed out of Russia to join our jury. We also invited the Russian-born pianist Nikita Magaloff, a Chopin specialist who was then living in Switzerland; the Hungarian pianist Géza Anda; the Austrian pianist and musicologist Paul Badura-Skoda, whose speciality was the Classical era; France's Yvonne Lefebure, a professor at the Paris Conservatoire who was an expert in the music of Debussy and Ravel; the Polish pianist and teacher Barbara Hesse-Bukowska, and Paul Huband from the BBC.

Inevitably, we did make a few mistakes at first. One was to disregard Sir Arthur Bliss's advice not to admit all applicants – it quickly became clear that some sort of initial selection process would in future be necessary, to weed out the no-hopers. A hundred and five competitors applied from thirty different countries as far afield as Colombia, Argentina, Poland, Russia, Australia and China, ranging in age from seventeen to twenty-eight. Of those, by far the greatest number – thirty-seven in all – were British. Around ninety competitors actually showed up. We had a few heart-stopping moments when the competitors did start arriving – the people coming from Russia and Poland, including two jurors and seven competitors, didn't turn up at Leeds City Station when they were expected, and we thought they might have been detained behind the Iron Curtain. But fortunately both contingents did arrive in time. Our other major omission was the lack of a properly thought-out marking system – we mistakenly thought, rather naively, that such internationally eminent and experienced jurors would prefer to evolve their own system. How wrong we were. Nikita Magaloff told us sternly that we must formulate rules for the Leeds International Piano Competition. At this point Geoffrey bravely stepped in, applied his logical mind to the problem, and devised a system of elimination based on 'one person, one vote' which has worked well at Leeds ever since and has been emulated by other competitions around the world. This system is applied until the final round, in which each juror votes for his or her preferred winner of each separate prize. We also decided that the same playing order (based on alphabetical surnames, after the opening player had been drawn by ballot) would be maintained until the final, in which musical considerations alone would determine the order of play.

Meanwhile our army of voluntary helpers had swung into action. We appointed a jury officer to shadow the jury members from the moment they arrived in Leeds to the moment they left, and to make sure they were always in the right place at the right time. They stayed at the Queens Hotel, so the chances of accidentally losing them were minimised. The competitors were fed and housed at Tetley Hall at the university, where Joan Valentine was in charge of the arrangements. She had to make sure that everyone was fed – often at different times of the day, depending on when they were scheduled to play – and all their different dietary requirements had to be taken into account. The transport arrangements were a nightmare. The competitors had to be allocated practice times – at least six hours a day if they wanted it – in houses all over Leeds, and we had to have a transport officer, who was responsible for arranging drivers to ferry them around and collect them. Our first transport officer was Betty Marcus, and she started off with just one car. And in days long before mobile phones were invented, it was very easy for the driver to get lost, especially in an unfamiliar district. The pianos available during the first round ranged from the most basic upright to a grand, and we tried to share out the best ones evenly.

The first week was the most chaotic – once the competitors had thinned out in the succeeding rounds, it became easier. The most important thing was that the competitors should arrive on time at the University for their performances. On the day of their performance, each competitor had to be brought down from Tetley Hall to the Great Hall of the University. They had to report to the Green Room three quarters of an hour before they were due to play. Each one was given half an hour on a practice piano to warm up, then Geoffrey, who acted as the platform announcer, checked the competitor's programme and its timings, and displayed them on a board in the hall with the name and nationality of the pianist. After the jury took its place, Geoffrey announced the competitor's name and the pieces he or she would play, and the competitor was ushered through the door on to the platform.

My former pupil Allan Schiller was the first competitor to sit down at the Steinway grand in the Great Hall of Leeds University at 10 a.m. on Friday, 13 September 1963, to start off the Leeds International Piano Competition. The second stage was to be held on Thursday and Friday, 19 and 20 September, which unhappily coincided with Yom Kippur, the Jewish Day of Atonement, the most solemn day in the Jewish calendar. Orthodox Jewish opinion was outraged; rabbis wrote in the *Jewish Gazette* that Jewish competitors and audience members would be better served attending synagogue than participating in a piano competition. I had to step in and point out that this was not the Leeds International *Jewish* Piano Competition, but as a result Jack Lyons and I were ostracised by local rabbis.

By and large, the standard of British entrants was low. Sir Arthur Bliss told the musical press that 'every time a British pianist appears on that platform, I want the floor to open and swallow me up'. Both Allan Schiller and my current pupil Michael Roll got through to the second round, but the list of disappointed candidates included John Barstow, who later became one of Britain's most prominent teachers, and the nineteen-year-old John Lill, who had already made his London début playing Rachmaninov's Third Concerto under Adrian Boult. He went on to take first prize in the 1970 Tchaikovsky Competition, and has had a brilliant career ever since.

As I had one current and one former pupil still in the competition, I felt it was necessary to keep a very low profile, so I stayed mainly at home, coaching Michael. I had been teaching him for eleven years, and now, at the age of seventeen, he was playing many of the great works by Mozart and Beethoven so beautifully that I thought I would enter him for the competition.

But he took it all far too casually. He was one of the youngest competitors. He had just left school that summer, and was planning to go to Leeds University to study medicine. He was mad about football, and instead of practising, he much preferred to kick a football around our garden with my eldest son Robert. A week before the competition started, he still hadn't learnt the compulsory test piece, *Notturno*. When he announced that he was planning to give up a whole Saturday afternoon to go to a Leeds United match rather than practise, I remember saying to him, 'If you go on like this, you'll disgrace me.'

On the day that Michael was due to play his first-round piece, Beethoven's *Appassionata* Sonata, I spent most of the day coaching him, before Geoffrey and I took him down to the Great Hall of the University. It was just like taking a soufflé out of the oven. He had risen to perfection. Other members of the jury told me that Sir Arthur Bliss wept, and Clifford Curzon said it was the finest performance he had ever heard. Michael chose to play Beethoven again in the second stage, this time the late Sonata in C minor, which is one of the most elusive and difficult.

I didn't attend any of the jury sessions. I stayed at home, and Marion reported to me on her return. Towards the end she said, 'You know, Michael is making a tremendous impression, and I think he's going to get right through to the finals', and so my reaction was one of great excitement.

On the Friday evening, the names of the finalists were announced. Instead of the three we expected, Sir Arthur Bliss announced that in view of the high standard of playing, there would be four finalists. They were the Frenchman Sebastien Risler; a twenty-seven-year-old New Yorker, Armenta Adams; a mercurial nineteen-year-old Russian student from the Moscow Conservatory called Vladimir Krainiev – and Michael Roll.

Michael opted to play the Schumann Concerto in the final. It was one he knew really well, having first played it in public when he was twelve, and then again several times since. But we still spent hours working on the first line of each phrase, to get it absolutely perfect.

On Finals Night, Leeds Town Hall was packed. It looked wonderful, decorated with the flags of the four competing nations, and the atmosphere was electric. Geoffrey and I sat with the Princess Royal, Marion and George Harewood, the Lord Mayor and Lady Mayoress of Leeds, the Bishop of Ripon and his wife, Sir Roger Stevens, the University's new Vice-Chancellor, and Sir Thomas Armstrong, Principal of the Royal Academy of Music. As well as Michael, Armenta Adams had opted to play the Schumann Concerto, while Risler chose Beethoven's Third, and Krainiev Liszt's brilliant E flat Concerto. The pressure of the event proved rather too much for Adams, who suffered an unfortunate memory lapse in the last movement of the Schumann, as so often happens with that piece, and Sebastien Risler's Beethoven was competent but rather dull. Krainiev's barnstorming Liszt certainly won over the audience, but Michael's musical account of the Schumann made a deep impression. The jury retired to consider its verdict. An hour went by, and tension rose in the hall. I was frantic with anxiety. I realised that if my own pupil were to win, against all the odds, it might do great harm to the competition's image. I begged Marion to intervene if necessary, and persuade the jury to award a joint first prize, but to no avail. The finalists were ushered back on to the platform, together with Sir Arthur Bliss. They had already been told the result, and as Sir Arthur began his summing up of the jury's decision, the mischievous Krainiev, from behind his back, showed the audience the result by holding up two fingers and pointing to himself, and then one, and pointing to Michael. When I went on to the platform to congratulate the finalists, I could sense the hostility in the hall, and felt very embarrassed.

Feelings certainly ran high. I remember that one of the members of the press had been approached afterward by a woman in the audience, who asked, 'Did you agree with the result?' And he said, 'Yes', whereupon she scratched his face. I told Sir Arthur that I thought that the result was rather unfortunate politically. 'Politics should never enter into music,' he replied.

The controversy over Michael's win rumbled on for several weeks. Sir Arthur felt obliged to defend the decision in a letter to the *Yorkshire Post*. Michael himself inflamed matters further when he declared that he still intended to study medicine, rather than embark on the uncertain life of a concert pianist. His parents supported his decision, but several members of the jury, and especially Jack and Roslyn Lyons, who had donated the prize money, were furious. John Pritchard remarked that it was a 'bit of a blow to the adjudicators and the patrons, seeing their cash used to fit a boy for a medical career'. Michael and his parents were thoroughly alarmed by the barrage of criticism and within twenty-four hours he announced that he had changed his mind. He withdrew his application to the Medical School, and continued to study with me for a few more years. He was signed up by a top agent and immediately got a handful of major engagements. Shortly after the competition I was encouraged to receive a letter from the great accompanist Gerald Moore, who wrote:

Dear Fanny Waterman

After listening on the radio yesterday to those two boys playing, I felt that the judges were absolutely right in awarding the palm to your pupil. Indeed I found the performance of the Schumann most moving and I felt I must write to express my deep admiration of the teaching you have given young Mr Roll. It is a great triumph for you and for this country and any British musician has had a moral and psychological boost out of it.

And Benjamin Britten wrote:

My dear Fanny Waterman,

May I congratulate you on the astounding and well-deserved success of Michael Roll? I am sure that a lot of it is due to your remarkable and tactful guidance of his talent – it cannot be easy to handle a gift of that size, & I think you have done it wonderfully. I hope he decides to make piano-playing his career – but I do understand his reluctance! . . . especially when one thinks of the careers of other prize winners. But I am sure with you to guide him he need have no fears. When I suggested him playing at the Festival next year I had no idea he would win the competition (having felt the Russian boy was a certainty). The invitation of course still stands – but I expect he will get other and bigger offers now, & we may have to be passed over if, indeed, he accepts any of them! Perhaps you would be kind & find out for us what he would like to do – we shall quite understand if he has bigger fish to fry!

It was a great pleasure to meet you again, & I do congratulate you on the real success of the competition.

With best wishes,
Yours sincerely,
BENJAMIN BRITTEN

How could he possibly have had bigger fish to fry?

9

Thoughts on Performing

Clifford Curzon once told me that he only needed to hear someone play three notes on the piano, and he could instantly tell whether they had any talent as a pianist.

Something makes people want to perform. I would never urge anyone on to the concert platform who does not wish to be there, and no teacher ever should. But for those who do want to perform, the only way to learn the job is to do it.

Life as a performing artist can be a bear-pit. I'm always reminded of a favourite joke of mine:

A talented but starving young pianist noticed that the circus was coming to town, so he rang the director asking for a job. 'Have you got any work for a poor, starving pianist?' he asked. 'I play a very fine *Mephisto Waltz.*' 'Sorry, I have no work for a pianist,' replied the director. A few days later, feeling even more hungry, he called the director again. 'I can play Liszt's *Campanella* if you prefer?' 'Sorry. There's still nothing I can offer you,' came the reply. The pianist made one last, desperate attempt to interest the director. 'I can play the *Mephisto Waltz* and *La Campanella* together, at the same time!' To which the director finally agreed: 'All right, come along.' But when the pianist turned up, he was told to don a bearskin, as the circus's performing bear was sick. The bear's act was to cross the ring on a tightrope, over a den of savage lions. 'I have nothing to lose,' thought the starving pianist, so he agreed to walk the tightrope. Halfway across, he lost his balance, and fell into the lions' den. 'My God, please save me!' he cried in desperation. Then came a whisper from one of the 'lions' next to him: 'Don't worry, we're all pianists!'

When I am asked what qualities a musician must possess to become a great performer, I say, 'First, you must have inclination and imagination, backed up by application, concentration and determination. There will be perspiration and at times frustration, even tribulation. But with inspiration you will receive appreciation and possibly adulation!'

Every great artist has their own individual sound. Many pianists can play very loudly, but there's something divine about really soft playing. Pianists like Radu Lupu, Murray Perahia, András Schiff, Mitsuko Uchida, all have the marvellous ability to play softly, and to create thousands of different tone-colours. When I hear a really great pianist, I feel like humbly falling on my knees to them. There is nobody I admire more than these great musicians. I admire singers in particular, because to reach the soul of the music they must not only have a beautiful voice, but a deep understanding of the poetry behind their songs, as well as a sympathetic accompanist.

The great composers, who reside with the gods, have left us their manuscripts as a personal legacy. Beethoven's 32 sonatas, Chopin's four Ballades, Bach's 48 Preludes and Fugues, for example, are the priceless inheritance of every pianist. But the manuscripts themselves are like Morse Code. They need a great artist to bring this code to life. The *score* is the point of departure, from childhood until their last recital. And then you get a spell of heaven on earth.

※

EVERY MUSICIAN SHOULD BE AWARE of fulfilling three roles when they play:

- The Performer, who plays a few phrases
- The Listener, who takes 'thinking time' between phrases to judge the sounds and silences they have produced
- The Critic, who assesses and analyses the playing. Was it too loud, too soft, too quick, too slow? Did the tone, the musical punctuation, the phrasing add up to their expressive

intention? Did the musician reach the soul of the composer? Finally, where was the magic?

Any performer must recognise that a performance is the sum total of what they play and must be communicated to the audience, to make the listener listen.

The great Russian teacher Heinrich Neuhaus said that in order to bring a performance to life, the artist should 'play our magnificent piano literature in such a way as to make the listener like it, to make him love life still more, make his feelings more intense, his longings more acute, and give greater depth to his understanding'.

A performance is the culminating experience of an artist's intensive work. Something extra happens during a performance that never happens during one's practice. A performance compels continuity, courage and greater concentration. And an audience is necessary to give the performer that vital inspiration and spontaneity. Without audiences to inspire great artists, concert halls will become empty. Music will not have a future, but only a past.

10

SIR WILLIAM 'CLUCK'!

I n spite of all the controversy over Michael Roll's win, the first
Leeds International Piano Competition had been a great success. We decided to hold the next one three years later, and from
that moment onwards, my life has been completely dominated by
the tsunami of work associated with the regular three-year cycle
of the Leeds.

Marion and I worked hard to secure an impressive list of
potential engagements for the 1966 winner, including a Prom and
a concert at the Royal Festival Hall, appearances at several major
British festivals including Edinburgh and Aldeburgh, and a BBC
broadcast recital and TV appearance. We also widened the repertoire requirements and introduced an extra stage, in which eight
semi-finalists would be selected to perform an own-choice recital
in Leeds Town Hall. From these, three finalists would perform a
concerto with the Royal Liverpool Philharmonic Orchestra under
Sir Charles Groves. This year Marion agreed to present the prizes,
as our first Patron, Princess Mary, had died the year before.

The jury for the second competition was one of the most distinguished we ever assembled. Its chairman was William Glock, a
former piano pupil of Schnabel, writer, critic, founder of the
Dartington Summer School, and Controller of Music at the BBC.
BBC Radio offered to record the semi-final stage and transmit
the recitals on the Music Programme, as well as broadcasting a
live radio transmission of the winners' concert from Leeds Town
Hall. And an energetic young producer with BBC Music and Arts,
John Drummond, proposed making a television documentary

about the competition, called *Great Expectations*. Its innovative style, which Drummond described as an 'eavesdropping documentary', involved competitors being interviewed and filmed at all the stages of the competition, not just when they were playing. Apart from his phenomenal musical knowledge, Drummond spoke seven languages, which proved a great asset when interviewing competitors, with whom he made friends. The programme was screened in October 1966 and achieved fantastic viewing figures for an artistic event. It won a production award at the Prague International Television Festival, and certainly helped Drummond's own career. He went on to run the Edinburgh Festival and eventually to become Controller of BBC Radio 3, the successor to the Music Programme. This was the start of the Leeds Competition's long association with BBC Radio and TV, and really helped us in terms of national and international exposure.

The other jury members in 1966 included Glock's friend and BBC colleague Hans Keller as vice-chairman, together with the American pianist and writer on music, Charles Rosen, and the pianists Gina Bachauer from Greece, Annie Fischer from Hungary, Rudolf Firkušný from Czechoslovakia, and the Russians Nikita Magaloff and Lev Oborin. The winner of the first Chopin Competition, Lev now taught piano at the Moscow Conservatory, where his pupils included Vladimir Ashkenazy. The intellectual distinction of this jury was further boosted by the great French teacher Nadia Boulanger, then seventy-nine years old. Her amazing roster of pupils had included some of the finest composers, pianists and conductors of the twentieth century: Aaron Copland, Elliott Carter, Igor Markevitch, Virgil Thomson, Dinu Lipatti and Daniel Barenboim. Nadia really was the international Queen of Music. She was tall, slim and distinguished, and she always wore long black dresses – she looked as if she didn't really belong in the twentieth century. She was renowned for a quality I have always admired – attention to detail. She once said, 'Anyone who acts without paying attention to what he is doing is wasting his life. He should pay the same attention to cleaning a window as to writing a masterpiece.'

Of course, all these people had strong artistic opinions and forceful personalities. Gina Bachauer rolled her eyes at other jury members and stuffed her handkerchief into her mouth to stop herself laughing out loud at the more grotesque interpretations. Her laughter was infectious, and at one point Geoffrey had to send a stern reprimand about the audible misbehaviour of the jury in the gallery. Since then, I have decided that the jury should sit downstairs in full view of the audience!

Every competition produces some contentious results with which some people don't agree. When you get fifteen people on a jury, they all have different artistic ideas, and each one is adamant that his or her opinion is the right one. Jury members shouldn't try to influence each other: their own personal opinions should be kept to themselves. I've always believed that 'if you have a secret to keep, you must keep it secret that you have a secret to keep'. When there are teachers on the jury with pupils in the competition, it is all too easy for those teachers to say to each other, 'I'll vote for yours if you vote for mine' – I've seen it happen all too often in other competitions, and I was determined that it wouldn't happen in ours. I do not wish anyone to be able to say of the Leeds, 'There has been any question regarding the integrity of the jury.'

We started with a total of ninety-one competitors, of whom fifteen were British. But over a third didn't show up, with no apology, much to the annoyance of the waiting team. The ones who did arrive included four Russians: three men, including Aleksei Nasedkin and a talented nineteen-year-old, Semyon Kruchin, and a very attractive twenty-four-year-old blond girl, Viktoria Postnikova. This time, it would be the Russians who caused the biggest controversy, although the fact that not one British pianist survived the first round caused some consternation in the press.

By the semi-final stage, it became obvious that the jury was divided. After a great deal of heated discussion, the jury decided that in view of the high standard of playing, five, rather than four, finalists should go through to the concerto stage. But as there was only one Finals Night, not everyone could play a complete concerto. In the end, we decided that two competitors would play the first movement of the Tchaikovsky, and the other two would play the remaining movements, with the first movement of the Brahms in the middle. It wasn't an ideal solution, but it was the best we could do.

The jury retired until there was a consensus. Finally, William Glock emerged to announce the result. He was emotionally drained with all the arguing. The winner was Orozco, with Postnikova and Kruchin sharing joint second place, Nasedkin third, and the Austrian Jean-Rodolphe Kars fourth. In his speech, Glock stressed that the decision was based on what the jury had heard at all stages of the competition.

After all the drama, the Lord Mayor of Leeds introduced an unintentional moment of light relief in his speech at the presentation ceremony. Princess Irene of Greece and Denmark (an excellent pianist who had studied with Gina Bachauer) found herself thanked for coming all the way from London. The Mayor then called on 'Sir William Cluck' (Glock) to give the results and referred to Marion as 'Marion of 'Arewood', and myself as 'Miss Fanny Water – Water – Waterhouseman'!

11

JOINING THE FABER FAMILY

Around the same time as the Leeds International Piano Competition was conceived, Marion and I started working on a piano tutor. She had attended her son David's lessons with me, and enjoyed seeing me in action as a teacher. By a coincidence, a short time later I was invited to Harewood with Geoffrey for a dinner. Benjamin Britten and Peter Pears were giving a song recital in Harrogate – Schubert's *Winterreise* – and they were staying with Marion. That morning, I had received a letter from the editor of a music publisher asking if I would consider writing a piano tutor, and I asked Ben at dinner if he had ever heard the name. He said no, but why didn't we think of approaching Faber Music. He had just left Boosey & Hawkes to join a new music publishing company attached to Faber & Faber. Donald Mitchell, who was a distinguished writer on music and a close friend of Ben, had been the editor of music books at Faber & Faber, and was now head of the new music company. Ben told us that he would talk to Donald about the project, and of course any suggestions that came from Ben were treated very seriously. We had produced a dummy with a few pictures, and after a while Faber Music decided to take it on. So it was through Ben that Marion and I were introduced to Faber Music, with whom we've been best-selling authors ever since. And that was how the *Waterman–Harewood Piano Series* came into being.

I put my own ideas and methods from my teaching experience into the tutor. The books were devised to represent a complete and developing year's work for a beginner, organised into Lessons, to help teachers. Scales, sight-reading, studies, rhythm and technical exercises, solo pieces and duets are all to be found in the one volume. Naturally it includes my own thoughts and suggestions as to how to approach technical problems such as fingering, but our focus, just as with the piano competition, was on musicality, and that was highly innovative. So for instance, we have a piece called 'Violin and Cello', in which the pianist's right hand represents a violin, and the left hand a cello, and if the pupil imagines what those instruments sound like, they will be encouraged to play with a singing tone, and very musically. In 'A Very Sad Story', I ask the pupil to think of something very sad when they are playing, in order to establish the right mood, and to tell the teacher what their story is about. What I aimed to do in the tutor was what I have always tried to do in my teaching – to open a child's mind and ears to music in an imaginative way, by finding the right imagery and way of expressing ideas. It aims to help the pupil to forget the tedium of practising, and begin to enjoy their lessons.

Each chapter deals with a technical or musical problem, and the scales, exercises and studies were carefully designed in steps to help the young pianist to master the pieces at the end of each chapter. Marion and I composed the early pieces, but we included an additional sequence of pieces by famous classical composers, including Bach's Minuet in G from the *Anna Magdalena Notebook*, a piece from Schumann's *Album for the Young*, and Beethoven's Sonatina in G, together with short studies by composers such as Gurlitt, Czerny and Burgmüller. We included an enlarged Note Chart at the end of the book to help both teachers and pupils with the basic task of note-learning, and a Star Chart, which rewards excellent progress throughout the week, and gives young children an incentive to keep on practising every day. This gentle 'bribery' can produce excellent results!

Marion's children, especially Jeremy, did some test-driving of the new tutor, and my younger son Paul contributed helpful suggestions. A young artist friend of Marion's contributed the original line drawings, and *First Year Piano Lessons with Fanny Waterman and Marion Harewood* was published in 1967. Marion and I were interviewed about the tutor on the BBC's Home Service *Talkabout* programme in June that year.

The new tutor was well reviewed, although it was felt that its rate of progression was quite fast for average young learners. But its style of presentation, which was much more up to date than any others of its time, was greatly praised. After Fabers took the bold step of reducing the price almost by half, it really took off. We soon realised that it needed more material in it at an earlier stage, so within about five years it had quite a radical makeover. Extra material was added, some of it based on Russian folk songs that no other Western tutors at that time were using. Robert Schumann understood the power of folk music. He wrote, 'Listen attentively to all folk songs; they are a treasure of beautiful melodies and will teach you the characteristics of different nations.' We also added in easy pieces by the great composers such as Bach, Mendelssohn, Mozart and Schumann, who wrote for the very young. After its re-vamp, *Piano Lessons* began to do very well, except in the USA, which proved a difficult market. The problem was that there were a fair number of entrenched piano methods on sale in the USA. In March 1982 I went to an American Music Teachers' National Association conference in Kansas City, and gave a major presentation and workshops there. All the American teachers flocked round me, wanting to glean ideas for their own teaching methods. After that I was invited to give many more lectures in America.

Once *First Year Piano Lessons* had established itself and was selling well, we brought out a sequel, *Second Year Piano Lessons*. That volume included material that addressed issues like the importance of good thumb-under technique, scale practice and sight-reading, but in an integrated way. That's what makes our tutors unique. At the beginning we included my Ten Musical Commandments for young pianists, intended to help them practise effectively. A third, more advanced book containing more repertoire appeared in 1973, at which time the title of the tutors was changed to *Piano Lessons Books I–III*. We also began to supplement the tutors by adding separate, carefully graded repertoire books. Then, in the mid-1980s, Faber suggested that we might like to think about compiling a tutor aimed at much younger beginners, in which the technical progression would move much more slowly. So we went back to the drawing board and came up with the *Me and My Piano* series, in a different format, with nursery rhymes that teach the rhythms and full colour illustrations aimed at younger children. That series also has associated repertoire books, ranging from nursery rhymes and Christmas carols to essential daily exercises, and has been a great success. The *Waterman–Harewood Piano Series* now encompasses 32 volumes, and almost 2 million copies have been sold all over the world.

12

THE DISTINGUISHED YEARS

By 1969 Marion had emerged from the trauma of her divorce and was making a new life for herself. She and I became joint Chairman of the competition's administrative committee. For the past two years we had enjoyed the support of a new local group of volunteers, the Friends of Leeds International Pianoforte Competition, who were dedicated to providing a solid base of financial support and practical assistance with the complicated job of running the competitions. Under my friend Lady Parkinson's chairmanship, they organised many fund-raising events, from recitals by previous Leeds contestants to parties and social events. Their efforts meant that they were able to donate £1000 toward the cost of the 1969 competition.

The prize money, as before, came from individual donors and local businesses, but the list of engagements we planned to offer the winner ranged from several radio and TV broadcasts and appearances at festivals including the Proms, to concerto dates with several British orchestras. These were the main attractions for the competitors. In addition, the BBC planned to record all the semifinal stages and the final concert for both radio and television.

When John Drummond, who was then Assistant Head of Music and Arts at the BBC, came up to consult with us on the proposed television coverage of the final, we felt we were being courted. After he left, Marion turned to me and said, 'We are now two very important ladies!' This year, the prizes would be presented by HRH the Duchess of Kent, a keen music-lover who herself came from a prominent Yorkshire family.

We asked William Glock to be chairman of the jury once more. He accepted, but said that the jurors should ideally not all be pianists themselves, so we made sure that some of the other members came from more varied backgrounds. They included the American violinist Szymon Goldberg and the English conductor Raymond Leppard.

Only twelve of the fifty-six entrants came from Britain, among them Howard Shelley, who is a fine pianist, Christopher Elton, and my former pupil Paul Crossley, who was at that time studying in Paris. The nine-strong French entry included Georges Pludermacher, a veteran of the first Leeds competition and Anne Queffélec, a first prize-winner at Munich in 1968. Six Americans entered, four Russians, including Emil Gilels's twenty-one-year-old daughter Elena, and three Brazilians. The youngest entrant was a fourteen-year-old Australian boy, Geoffrey Tozer. But the name that stood out from the start was Radu Lupu, a twenty-three-year-old Romanian who had studied with Neuhaus in Moscow, and had won the second Van Cliburn competition in 1966. He had already made his Carnegie Hall debut, and had recently played all five Beethoven concertos in Bucharest. Lupu was clearly on his way to an international career, but was developing a reputation for being temperamental. From the minute he arrived in Leeds, he caused some alarm among the other contestants by practising concertos while all the others were working on perfecting their first-round pieces.

There was, however, a very comradely spirit among the contestants that year. Radu Lupu and Georges Pludermacher spent quite a lot of time playing either table tennis or four-hand arrangements of Beethoven symphonies when they weren't actually competing. They both went through to the semi-final, together with Queffélec, Tozer, Moreira-Lima, and three of the four Russians. Radu Lupu nearly refused to play his semi-final recital because a suitable warm-up piano wasn't available in the practice room, but he gave way and delivered a brilliant performance of the four Schubert Impromptus and Beethoven's *Waldstein* Sonata.

After the semi-final stage, there was very nearly a major upset. The jury members voted for the three allocated places in the finals, and both French contestants, together with Moreira-Lima, went safely through. But Radu Lupu and the Russian Boris Petrushansky were fourth and fifth on the list, and it looked at first as if neither would get through to the final. Although I myself was not a jury member, I made my feelings known in the strongest possible terms that the omission of these fine pianists would be a grave mistake and a blot on the history of the competition. At first some jury members – including Clifford Curzon, who favoured Pludermacher – refused to reconsider, but eventually the rest of the jury was persuaded to admit five finalists, rather than three.

However, there was still only one Finals Night, and again all five couldn't play a complete concerto. Lupu sent a message to the jury saying, 'Which of the Beethoven concertos would you like me to play?' The jury declined to make his choice for him, and eventually he settled on the first movement of the Third. Petrushansky chose the first movement of the Fourth, Arthur Moreira-Lima chose the second movement of Chopin's No. 2, Pludermacher the first and second movements of Brahms No. 2, and Anne Queffélec the last two movements of Bartók No. 3. Anne was very miserable throughout the competition, as her mother was very ill at the time, and in fact died shortly afterwards. Boris Petrushansky had been stung on one of his fingers by a wasp on the afternoon of the final, and Geoffrey had to give him a pain-killing injection, but it may have affected his performance to some extent. The star of the show was undoubtedly Radu Lupu, whose Beethoven was truly spectacular. Later, I overheard Clifford Curzon, who had been against admitting Lupu to the final at all, putting his hands together in prayer and saying, 'Thanks be to God that I heard that performance.' 'But, Clifford,' I said, 'you didn't originally vote for him.' To which Clifford replied, 'No, because I was so sure he would get through that I voted for a dark horse instead.'

This time, the jury's verdict was almost unanimous. The Leeds International Piano Competition had gained its first superstar winner in Radu Lupu, who has gone on to become one of the greatest pianists of our time.

⚹

OUR GREATEST WORRY at the end of the 1969 competition was money. Where were we going to find enough to keep it all going? I felt it was humiliating that I should have to go begging for funds for an event of such calibre. Our voluntary helpers were putting in a magnificent effort, but we did now need a proper office and professional secretarial help.

The Friends of the Leeds International Piano Competition somehow managed to raise most of the money to keep the competition going. Some financial help also came from the Leeds Corporation and the University, together with the Arts Council of Great Britain and the Yorkshire Arts Association. The Duchess of Kent, who had presented the prizes at the 1969 competition, became our Patron, while the president was still the Lord Mayor of Leeds. There were now six vice-presidents, including Lord Boyle of Handsworth, who in 1970 succeeded Sir Roger Stevens as Vice-Chancellor of Leeds University. For the next decade, until his untimely death from cancer, Edward Boyle was one of the greatest supporters of the competition, as well as one of Geoffrey's and my dearest friends.

Lord Boyle had been MP for the Handsworth constituency in Birmingham for over twenty years, until he retired from politics in 1970. Watching the Leeds International Piano Competition on television played a major part in his decision to give up politics and move to Leeds as Vice-Chancellor of the University, a move he never regretted.

He had been a popular member of the Cabinet in the Macmillan government as Secretary of State for Education and Science, and was greatly liked and respected by his former colleagues as a man who had entered public life for the good of the country. His incredibly wide knowledge of cultural and educational affairs made him an ideal university Vice-Chancellor,

81

while his passions and enthusiasms included history, philosophy, cricket, and especially music. Both his parents had been music-lovers, and his own musical tastes ranged from Monteverdi to Tippett, though his favourite composers were Mozart and Fauré. His profound knowledge and love of music, together with his political expertise and diplomatic skills seemed to Geoffrey and myself to make him an ideal choice as chairman of the competition's jury. So we approached him, and he acted in that capacity for the next three competitions. He gave us so much prestige. He guaranteed the continuation of the University's support for the competition, and the use of its facilities.

As an active chairman of the jury, with full voting powers, Edward took a keen interest in the administration of the competition. He came to our meetings and helped Geoffrey and myself choose repertoire. I can think of no one who knew more about music. He spent hours listening to different recordings of the pieces, and studying scores. His amazingly retentive memory allowed him to discuss the competitors' performances with them without ever having to refer to his notes – he could remember exactly what each one had played in the greatest detail, and how. We never had any problems on the jury when Edward Boyle was there. As soon as he opened his mouth, everyone was silent. Nobody would do or say anything improper to Edward Boyle. When I listen to discussions in Parliament today, I feel very sorry that there aren't more people like him.

Wherever I went, everyone wanted to speak to Edward. He was much in demand at parties, but if he was trapped by a 'party bore' and needed to be extricated from a tedious conversation, he and I devised a secret plan. If he adjusted his tie, he was sending me a message that said, 'Save me!' Whatever subject was raised, he knew more about it than anyone, even the experts. His astounding breadth of knowledge did make everyone very nervous, but when he was addressing you, he spoke as if you understood every word he was saying. Usually, after two or three minutes, I would be completely lost and couldn't follow him. He could be talking about fifteenth-century Rome, looking you in the face, and you would be far too embarrassed to say, 'Stop, Edward, I really don't know what you are talking about!' He left you behind with his vast knowledge, and yet you found you agreed with every word he said – he was so convincing!

The other members of the 1972 jury included four people who had served in 1969 as well as five other distinguished European pianists. In view of her advanced age, and the fact that she was losing her sight, I invited Nadia Boulanger to be an 'honorary onlooker', but she replied, 'If I come to Leeds I would prefer not to come as a guest, but I would like to be on the jury.' No doubt remembering the rumpus during the 1966 competition, she added that it would be on the strict condition 'that there is no discussion when a jury goes into the room to cast their vote. That should be done in absolute silence.'

I had a phone call on the afternoon that the sessions were due to start. It was Nadia, saying, 'I'm at Leeds City Station, and no-body is here to meet me.' As no one else was available, I rang up Lord Edward Boyle. He stopped what he was doing, went down to the station, and collected her. During the competition she said to me, 'Miss Waterman, I want to ask you a very personal question. Who is Edward Boyle?' I said, 'He was the Minister of Education, and is now Vice-Chancellor of the University of Leeds, and an excellent scholar.' She said, 'But he is also a very *great* musician.' On the last evening of the competition, at the Town Hall, Leeds University honoured Nadia with the award of an Honorary Doctorate to mark her eighty-fifth birthday. It was the last time she visited Leeds. Shortly after the end of the competition, she sent a touching letter congratulating me on the success of 'this unthinkable adventure', and adding, in her inimitable way, that she thought I might like to know that she had arrived safely in London, where she was staying with Yehudi Menuhin, and that the flowers we had given her on the last night of the competition were still fresh. She hoped they stay alive forever to remind her of her happiness in Leeds.

We had a huge response in 1972, and for the first time we had to cut down the initial entries, from 188 to 95. However, only 59 actually turned up to play. But once again, the standard was so high that twenty competitors, four more than originally planned, went through to the second round. They included an eighteen-year-old Hungarian named András Schiff, and Mitsuko Uchida, a twenty-three-year-old Japanese who had studied in Vienna.

Just before the competition started, I had a phone call from the American businessman and philanthropist Irving Moskovitz, whom we had met while holidaying in the South of France. 'Please book me a room at the best hotel in Leeds,' said Moskovitz. 'I'm coming over from New York, and I'm bringing the winner with me.' 'How do you mean?' I said, sceptically. 'Well, if he doesn't win, I want to be there to hear the pianist who beats him,' said Moskovitz. His protégé turned out to be Murray Perahia, a twenty-five-year-old American whose rising reputation already sent shivers down his rivals' backs. Perahia was so thoroughly rehearsed that during the first stage of the competition he claimed he just rested and looked over the scores of his first-round choices rather than practising. In the second round, his deeply moving performance of Schumann's *Davids-bündlertänze* reduced several members of the jury to tears – people walked out holding handkerchiefs to their eyes. I don't remember another occasion before or since when everyone was so moved. Mitsuko Uchida also chose to play the *Davids-bündlertänze*, and both she and Perahia got through to the semi-final, together with three other Americans, including Craig Sheppard and Eugene Indjic.

At this point, Ladbrokes opened a book on the semi-finalists, offering odds of 7–4 against the favourite, Murray Perahia. Some-one placed a bet of £1000 on him. The other competitors were upset and angry when they found out – they said it made them feel like racehorses. I knew nothing about betting, and as an ignoramus, I innocently asked, 'Who is *writing* the book?' Word was also getting round that there was a startling new talent in the making, and several major London agents were starting to nose around Perahia.

In the end, we had an all-American final. The voting had been so clear-cut that at least the audience would, for the first time, be treated to three complete concertos. For Finals Night, both Indjic and Sheppard chose the Rachmaninov Third, traditionally a great warhorse concerto, while Murray Perahia opted for Chopin's No. 1. The final became a duel between Sheppard's technically brilliant Rachmaninov, and Perahia's poetic Chopin. On the basis of the concertos alone, some critics and audience members thought that Sheppard should have won. But as the judges had heard all the performances throughout the competition, Murray Perahia – whom Nadia Boulanger described as 'a poet coming to light' – had shown himself to be an outstanding musician and an exceptional and worthy artist. When I look back on that year, I realise how honoured we were that he decided to enter.

Murray himself sent me the following letter:

Dear Miss Waterman

I wish to thank you so much for the very thoughtful and considerate way you ran and organised the competition, and for your very personal and human interest, not only in myself but, I think, in all the competitors.

I think you very much succeeded in your goal of taking the competitive part out of the competition. And as a result, both the musical motivation and direction (shown by both the choice of repertoire and also the choice of jury) of the competition, was one that I regard very highly.

It was also wonderful speaking to you & I look forward to our next meeting.

Best regards,
Murray Perahia

And after hearing Murray give his winner's début recital in the Queen Elizabeth Hall, Clifford Curzon wrote me a letter which I have treasured ever since, and which I hope sums up the essence of the Leeds Competition:

What greater and more touching pleasure is there in life than giving a young and beautiful talent a little lift in the direction (only, for we can never reach them) of the stars?

That is the ethos of our competition.

%

IT WAS AFTER MURRAY'S RECITAL at the Queen Elizabeth Hall in September that Marion's name became linked with the politician Jeremy Thorpe. They had been introduced a few months earlier by Moura Lympany. Marion asked to sit next to Jeremy at Murray's concert, and that was the first time we realised that she was seriously interested in him. Her life was about to change completely – but unknown to her, it was a case of 'out of the frying pan, into the fire'.

Jeremy Thorpe was the MP for North Devon and the leader of the Parliamentary Liberal Party. When he was elected in 1959, there were so few Liberal MPs that people joked that they could hold their meetings in the back of a London taxi – which in the light of recent political events, is beginning to look all too relevant again! Jeremy was also a widower with an infant son, Rupert, having lost his young wife in a road accident after only two years of marriage. It was easy to see why Marion was attracted to him. He was handsome, charismatic and ambitious, and he had a wicked sense of humour. He made everybody laugh. But what nobody outside a close circle of parliamentary colleagues knew at the time was that he had an extremely colourful private life. For years he had had a string of male lovers from all walks of society, and his colleagues were becoming very concerned about his indiscretions. Rumours were beginning to circulate around Parliament and elsewhere.

Jeremy proposed to Marion in February 1973. Geoffrey and I were told to keep the date of their wedding a secret to avoid publicity. They were married very quietly at Paddington Register Office on 14 March and afterwards had their marriage blessed in

Westminster Abbey, followed by a luncheon party for their close friends in the Jerusalem Chamber at the Abbey. As her greatest friends, Marion invited Geoffrey and myself, as well as Benjamin Britten and Peter Pears. By then Ben was very ill with heart problems: he had an operation not long afterwards from which he never really recovered. In July that year Geoffrey and I were among a thousand guests invited to a lavish party at Covent Garden to celebrate their marriage, with a champagne reception and a concert given by some of their musician friends. Janet Baker sang Schubert and Handel, Yehudi and Hepzibah Menuhin played Beethoven's 'Spring' Sonata, and Murray Perahia and Clifford Curzon played a Mozart sonata for two pianos. It was a wonderful occasion.

At first, Marion and Jeremy seemed very happy together. They shared a love of music, and although Marion wasn't a political animal, she adapted very quickly to being the wife of a politician, and stepmother to Jeremy's young son, Rupert. But by now she and Jeremy were dividing their time between their London home and his Devon constituency, and visited Leeds only rarely. We were seeing each other less often. Nevertheless in 1974 Marion and I decided to launch another venture – the Leeds National Musicians' Platform. We intended it to be a non-competitive event to showcase young performers, including chamber music ensembles, and to give them a chance to display their talents to agents and concert promoters. The preliminary rounds would be held in London, and only the final concerts would be held in Leeds. But it very quickly turned into a competition in all but name – for the second event in 1977 Lloyds Bank donated a 'prize' of £500, and by the third time it was held, in 1980, it had accrued a huge panel of 'assessors', plus semi-final recitals in Leeds University's Great Hall, and a concerto final with the Philharmonia Orchestra in the Town Hall. In 1980 our finalists were an oboist, a baritone, a clarinettist and a piano trio (who had to perform Beethoven's Triple Concerto). Although the Leeds National Musicians' Platform did encourage the careers of some outstanding British players, including the cellists Caroline Dale and Steven Isserlis, the harpsichordist Melvyn Tan, the flautist Philippa Davies, the clarinettist Michael Collins and my daughter-in-law, Vanya Milanova, the 1980 event was the last of its kind, as it proved increasingly difficult and time-consuming to attract sufficient funding.

The year 1974 proved to be the high point of Jeremy Thorpe's political career. In February that year, the beleaguered Prime Minister, Edward Heath, having been forced to inflict the miseries of the three-day working week on the nation, and faced with a damaging miners' strike, called a general election. The Liberal Party fielded 517 candidates, many more than ever before, and the party achieved over 6 million votes – which unfortunately translated into only 14 seats in the House of Commons. Jeremy's personal approval rating with the public was sky high – much higher than either of his opponents. But the voters had delivered a hung parliament, with the Conservatives winning four fewer seats than Labour, and for five days Jeremy Thorpe's Liberal Party held the balance of power, with Heath offering Jeremy the possibility of joining him in a coalition, with a cabinet seat. Marion and he were so excited about it. But the party was less keen, and after intense discussions, Jeremy decided to reject Heath's offer. Heath resigned, and Harold Wilson became Prime Minister. Jeremy had missed his chance of high government office, much to his disappointment.

After Edward Heath had resigned, he spent time writing his memoirs. Not long after *Sailing: A Course of My Life* appeared in 1975, I received an unexpected phone call from Edward Heath's private secretary, asking if I might like to meet the former prime minister. I was amazed at the question (and for a moment thought someone was pulling my leg). I responded immediately, however, that I would be delighted. He invited himself to tea at our house, and the Trustees of the Piano Competition joined us. Music was one of Edward Heath's greatest passions in life. He was a close friend of Moura Lympany, and had installed a Steinway grand piano in 10 Downing Street during his premiership. When he saw my two grand pianos, he said, 'Let's play together!' We sat down and played *Jesu, Joy of Man's Desiring*. Later on he asked for

Receiving my CBE with Geoffrey

With Sir Simon Rattle

Dame Janet Baker   Sir Mark Elder
(photograph by Simon Dodd)

At home with my pianos

Receiving my DBE with Robert, Lara and Paul

With John Major   With The Prince of Wales,
                   Patron of the Harrogate Festival

Lord John Dyson   Harvey McGregor

With Marion and Dame Janet, and Sarah Jane and Gordon Brown

With the Lord Chief Justice   With Karin Pfautsch, lifelong friend
Peter Taylor and his wife

With Benjamin Frith   With András Schiff

With Radu Lupu   With Federico Colli

With Sir David Tang and Lang Lang
(photograph by Christine van de Merwe)

With my recent pupils

Granddaughter Carmella, with husband Erion and son Leart

With my son Robert and his daughters

a suggestion of where he could go out to dinner. Geoffrey presumed he would want somewhere quiet, but he requested a busy restaurant where people would recognise him and shake him by the hand. Edward Heath was the first of what I call 'my Three Prime Ministers' – the ones I have known personally. The others are John Major, whom we met at official receptions, and Gordon Brown, who, together with his wife Sarah, took a great interest in my work with disadvantaged children.

%

LORD BOYLE AGAIN AGREED TO CHAIR THE JURY for the 1975 competition. The newcomers that year included Rosalyn Tureck, who at that time was considered to be the world's greatest Bach specialist. For the first time, there would be two consecutive Finals Nights, giving six competitors the chance to play a complete concerto with the Royal Liverpool Philharmonic Orchestra under Sir Charles Groves. This year, the semi-finals and the finals were held in the Grand Theatre, as the Town Hall was closed for repairs. BBC Television arranged to broadcast the whole of the Saturday evening final live from the theatre, together with recorded highlights from the Friday night final.

Several of the seventy-two competitors had entered before, including András Schiff, Mitsuko Uchida and Geoffrey Tozer, now in his mid-twenties. The fact that they re-entered showed that they had absolute confidence in the integrity of our voting system. The Russians sent three pianists, including Dmitri Alexeev, a first prize-winner at the Enescu Competition in Bucharest. My pupil Jonathan Dunsby was the only British pianist to reach the second round.

Alexeev, Uchida, the Frenchman Pascal Devoyon and Schiff were among the eight semi-finalists. All four went through to the final, in which Schiff played a Bach concerto, Uchida the Schumann, Devoyon chose Beethoven's Fourth, and Dmitri Alexeev gave a dazzling performance of Prokofiev's Third Concerto. What a standard it was!

For once, the jury delivered a unanimous verdict on the first prize, which looking back seems extraordinary, given the wealth of talent on display that year. Dmitri Alexeev was declared the winner, with Uchida second, and Schiff and Devoyon joint third. András Schiff was very disappointed. He had played Bach in both the semi-final and final rounds, and thought that Rosalyn Tureck may have taken against his interpretations. It caused a certain coolness between us for several years. But the jury does not have access to a crystal ball. Sir András Schiff is undoubtedly one of the world's greatest pianists. I attended a recent recital of his at which he played Bach's Goldberg Variations in one half, and Beethoven's Diabelli Variations in the other. It was sensational.

The Leeds International Piano Competition had this time uncovered not just one, but several world-class pianists. It was now truly the world's leading piano competition.

13

JURY SERVICE

The world is a country which nobody ever yet knew by description:
one must travel through it one's self to be acquainted with it.

LORD CHESTERFIELD

When I was eight, my mother once said, 'One day, I will travel the world with you.' Sadly, she never did – but her vision was remarkable. Since then, I have travelled all over the world giving masterclasses, and especially as a juror on international competitions.

I was first proposed as a juror on the 1977 Beethoven Competition in Vienna by Alfred Brendel, and I was deeply honoured to be received by such a great artist. I wanted to live up to his high standards. I enjoyed that competition, as who wouldn't enjoy listening to so much Beethoven? I also enjoyed meeting the other musicians with whom I worked. At first I was mostly invited to European competitions, but during the 1980s I went to the USA, South America, South Africa, Israel and Russia, and from the 1990s, also to the Far East, China and Korea. I went to the Tchaikovsky Competition for the first time in 1986. It was a very moving experience for me personally. My father had died two years earlier, and as I sat on the stage at the Bolshoi in Moscow I thought about the Ukrainian village he had come from. I felt he was looking down on me, and that the wheel had come full circle.

My mother never did travel the world with me, but Geoffrey usually took his holidays to coincide with my trips abroad. He loved it – we were taken to some wonderful places, and he could go round and greet all the competitors he had originally met in Leeds, whom he knew better than I did as chairman. There was a real party atmosphere at the Tchaikovsky Competition – everyone stays up all night eating caviar and drinking vodka. Some people find the pace rather hard to take! I have been several times on the jury of the Dublin Competition, and that also has a very convivial atmosphere. My travels all over the world have also made me open-minded and tolerant of other people's politics, religion and culture.

I'm like a musical spy. When I sit on juries, I form an opinion as to whether I think other members would be fair, honest and have the musical wisdom and stamina to serve on our Leeds jury. I also look for people with wide genuine musical knowledge, as I think juries should be composed not only of fine pianists and teachers, but also of composers and conductors. My work as an international juror also gives me the opportunity to hear many fine, up-and-coming young pianists, and if I think they show real promise, I suggest, after the competition has concluded, that they might consider applying to Leeds.

What is a competition jury looking for? Three fundamental things – craftsmanship, musicianship, and artistry. The last of these is the rarest. It encompasses musical integrity – adherence to a score and the composer's instructions; rhythmic vitality – the subtle variations, including rubato, that give life to the rhythm and lets a melody soar; beauty of tone – how to make the piano, which is basically a percussive instrument, sing; and lastly, that indefinable quality called magic, imagination, or inspiration, which makes the audience sit up and listen.

One's function as a jury member is not only to be knowledgeable, but also distinguished. We do not behave as MPs do currently, with everybody shouting over everyone else. This is what's going wrong with politics at the moment. We should all show respect for each other.

Good jurors do tend to get invited back to many competitions. But that can be dangerous, as one could be perceived to be doing it for personal advantage and one's own agenda. For many years the jury at Leeds was invited on a voluntary basis, receiving only accommodation and travel expenses, but since 1990 we have had to bow to the inevitable and offer a fee, in line with other international competitions.

What makes the Leeds competition so unique? It's because of its integrity. We publish the rules in our brochure, so that everybody can see how the competitors are to be judged. Competitors know that if they come to the Leeds they will get a fair deal. But I'm sorry to say that elsewhere that is not always the case. I get very worked up when I see injustice, but I try to behave as calmly as I can. I have come across horse-trading: I've heard deals made – 'If you vote for X, I'll vote for Y' – to which I reply, 'I'm not bribable.' It's very worrying if that develops during a competition. They're gambling with young musical lives. One has occasionally heard of a certain kind of bribery in some competitions, but fortunately that's quite rare. I once heard a story told by another juror of how the family of one competitor had sent a Model B Steinway to be installed in the studio of one of the professors who was on a competition jury. That kind of behaviour has never happened at Leeds.

Some jurors are not really fit for purpose. I was once serving on the jury for the Queen's Prize at the Royal College of Music in London, flanked by two eminent colleagues. One candidate started playing the last movement of Beethoven's *Appassionata* Sonata too fast for the composer's marking. I was surprised, and turned to my colleague on the right, saying, 'Don't you think that's too fast for allegro moderato?' To which he replied, 'I'm sorry? I'm deaf in my left ear.' I was so astonished that I turned to my left and whispered to my neighbour, 'He says he's deaf in his left ear', to which the second juror responded, 'I'm deaf in my right.'

Being the chairman of a jury is a responsible and arduous position. You must keep your jury happy and try to avoid lobbying. I don't want any political voting by the Leeds jury. The chairman should discourage discussion, as Nadia Boulanger said, otherwise the most eloquent advocates influence the others, especially the weaker ones. Discussions lead only to acrimony. Two or three jurors will always get together and try to influence each other – when they are not playing bridge! It becomes like a football game. The sooner you get down to voting, the better. No one at Leeds knows how other jury members have voted – not even me. It's part of our rules that after the votes there's no discussion about the results. Once the vote has taken place, the votes are counted in the presence of the jury. I am informed of the result and read it out. When I read out the names, they're in alphabetical order. There are no clues there to the actual marks each player has received, nor their position. Not only is fair play done, but it has to be seen to be done. The system we developed at Leeds is respected around the world, and other competition organisers have followed our example.

Some juries seem to gel better than others – it all depends on the personalities involved. You always get someone who's a troublemaker and someone who's a peacemaker. When any small group of people is thrown together – working and eating together – for a lengthy period of time, tempers naturally get quite frayed. Listening to music is such an intense experience. People switch on and off, and come out of each session absolutely drained. I remember in one afternoon at the 1987 Leeds competition, we had to listen to seven consecutive performances of *Gaspard de la nuit*, followed by seven more of Brahms's G major Violin Sonata with poor Erich Gruenberg. Another time we had to listen to more performances of Prokofiev's Third Sonata than was comfortable, and at the 1990 final, four out of six competitors chose to play the Schumann Concerto. It can be absolutely gruelling. But really it's up to the chairman to try to unite everyone. I have been called 'Field Marshal Fanny', and while I am still chairman of the Leeds jury, I intend to keep everything under control.

At Leeds, our prime concern is for the competitors. Once, our administrative helpers mistakenly put jury members in seats allocated to competitors at the winners' gala recital, telling the jury members that they were more important. I said to the administrators, 'Excuse me, you are in no position to do that. If a member of the jury dropped out, he or she could be replaced within twenty-four hours. But if the competitors don't come, then we will have a poor entry, and the competition's reputation will be harmed.'

Over recent years we have had some outstanding jurors at Leeds. One of these was the veteran Chinese pianist and teacher Zhou Guangren. She overcame great tribulation, including serious damage to her hands while being forced to work in the fields during the Cultural Revolution, and again when a piano collapsed on her. Despite her injuries, she managed to play again. Her courage is an inspiration to us all. She has served on several of the Leeds juries during the past two decades, and is greatly beloved.

It's quite rare for a jury to reach a unanimous decision – it hasn't happened very often at Leeds. And there certainly have been some lively disagreements. But we like to feel we're a civilised group of people who respect each other and the competitors, and are able to see the other's point of view.

INTERLUDE II
FAVOURITE JOKES AND ANECDOTES

I have always loved jokes, and this is a selection of some of my favourites.

A conductor was doing *Messiah*, and in the famous pause in the Hallelujah Chorus, just before the final cadence, a voice was heard from the front row of the audience saying loudly, 'I know what *you* like, but I like *mine* fried with onions!'

⅜

AN IRISHMAN HAD DIED, and as is customary, his neighbours and friends came round for the wake, to commiserate with the widow as he lay in his coffin in the front room for all to see. With such comments as 'Oh, he was a grand man!' they keened. 'Oh, he was very popular.' 'Oh, he was so handsome!' Then the last one said, 'And he looks *so* well!' 'And so he should!' said the widow. 'He's just come back from a two-week holiday in Blackpool!'

⅜

TWO LADIES IN TEL AVIV had just finished their lunch. The waiter came up to settle the bill, and he said to them, 'Was *anything* all right?'

⅜

A MAN COMES HOME TO HIS WIFE, and says, 'You'll probably be very upset, but I ought to tell you that I've got a mistress. Don't worry, I'll still be here at the weekends, but during the week I'll be living with her.' The weekend arrives, and he takes his wife to the theatre. He scans the gallery with his binoculars and then starts waving to someone. His wife says, 'Who's that?' Her husband replies, 'That's my mistress.' His wife grabs the binoculars, has a good look, and then hands them back with a shrug and a snub: 'So what?' The next weekend the same thing happens. Her husband waves again. 'Who are you waving to now?' says his wife. 'I never told you before, as it's none of my business,' says her husband. 'Max, my business partner, also has a mistress, and she's up there in the gallery.' 'Give me the binoculars!' says his wife once again. She snatches them, takes a long look, and then digs her husband in the ribs with a satisfied smile. '*Ours* is nicer!'

⚹

I WAS GIVING MY WINDOW-CLEANER a mug of tea. I asked him if he was married. He answered, 'I was, but my wife died.' To show my sympathy, I replied, 'I'm terribly sorry to hear that. What did she die from?'

'Oh, nothing serious!'

⚹

A PROUD MOTHER AND FATHER are watching their soldier son on the parade ground during the Trooping the Colour ceremony. Suddenly he stumbles. The mother says anxiously, 'Our Charlie isn't keeping time with the rest!' 'You're wrong,' says the father. 'Everybody else is out of step with our Charlie!'

⚹

GEOFFREY AND I ONCE WROTE to British Rail to complain about bad service we had encountered, and were rather annoyed to receive a curt standard letter thanking us for drawing the matter to their attention, etc. A friend of ours to whom we related our tale of woe sent us this anecdote:

It is alleged that a traveller on the Canadian-Pacific Railway who spent a night in a sleeping-car was bitten by a bedbug. He wrote a letter of complaint to the company, and in due course received a reply from a man describing himself as 'Manager of Passenger Services'. It read:

Dear Sir,

We were dismayed and appalled to receive your letter of complaint, a copy of which I enclose for your convenience of reference. Such a thing has never before happened in the history of our company, and we have taken drastic steps to ensure it does not happen again. We have traced the coach in which you travelled. The bed linen had already been sent to the laundry, where our standard process of successive washes in mild insecticidal solution, boiling soapy water, and pure water from our own Rocky Mountain spring will ensure its absolute cleanliness and freedom from any chemical irritant. Furthermore, in our determination to remove the slightest risk of a further complaint, we have stripped the entire coach of all upholstery, carpets and woodwork; all this has been burned. The bare metal of the coach has then been sprayed, under high pressure, with a powerful insecticide and then with two applications of pure spring water. The coach is now being rebuilt, and we feel confident that neither it nor any other of our rolling stock, all of which is being given careful inspection, will fall short of our hitherto irreproachable standard of clinical cleanliness.

Yours very truly . . .

Unfortunately, the confidence of the recipient was somewhat dented by the fact that the secretary who photocopied the original letter of complaint did not notice that on the copy sent back to the complainant, someone had written across the top, 'Send this BF a copy of Bed-Bug Letter No. 2.'

❋

I love a laugh and a giggle. These jokes and anecdotes have served me well over the years, and I still laugh at them. I hope you enjoy them as much as I do.

14

PIANO PROGRESS

My life as a performing musician had not equipped me with business acumen, but as the growing reputation of the Leeds International Piano Competition brought me into contact with wealthy and influential people from the business world, I took the opportunity to ask them if they might be interested in sponsoring the competition. After the 1975 competition I was visiting my cousin, Dr Harold Waterman, in Leicester, and was invited to have lunch with Sir Mark Henig, Chairman of the British Tourist Board, and a former Lord Mayor of Leicester. As we were leaving, he asked if there was anything he could do to help us. I mentioned that we were looking for sponsorship for the Leeds International Piano Competition, and the next day I had a phone call arranging a meeting for Marion and myself with Robin Frost, who handled PR for Harveys of Bristol, the wine importers. We arrived late at the meeting and were totally unprepared as to what we were going to say as regards facts and figures. He asked us, 'How much money do you need?' and we didn't know the answer. We looked at each other afterwards and Marion said, 'A fine mess you've got us into!' However, the very next day I had a phone call to say that Harveys wanted to be associated with the competition. Clearly, after meeting us, they had faith that their sponsorship would be used wisely, and not wasted. Robin Frost was a real gentleman and a delight to work with. He truly had the interests of the competition at heart. Our association with Harveys lasted until 1993, and gave us some much-needed financial stability. One of the conditions was that the competition should carry the firm's name. This caused a few problems during the 1980s with the BBC over its strict policy of not including commercial sponsors' brand names on air or within sight of television cameras. Our committee was very dubious about attaching a brand name to the competition, but my own view was 'Take it or leave it!'

The relationship between the arts world and commercial sponsors has always been a thorny one. Once, artists such as Piatigorsky, Milstein and Horowitz had to rely on enterprising impresarios or individual agents such as Emmie Tillett who were willing to take a risk to sponsor them at the beginning of their careers, but it has become increasingly difficult for young artists to find agents willing to take them on – unless they win a major competition. In the UK, the BBC has done much to promote young careers, with BBC Young Musician of the Year, Cardiff Singer of the World, Young Dancer of the Year, and especially its excellent Young Generation Artists programme. Several former Leeds prizewinners have appeared on this scheme. The role of the BBC in promoting the careers of young artists in this country cannot be praised enough.

Our new sponsorship deal with Harveys meant that in 1978 we were able to increase the Leeds prize money for the first time since 1966. The BBC agreed to televise both Finals Nights live and in full, together with the prize-giving ceremony and selected highlights from the semi-final round.

Lord Boyle again chaired the 1978 jury, which apart from Artur Balsam and Phyllis Sellick, was entirely new. This year the semi-finals included a chamber-music stage, in which the competitors had to perform a chamber work with the Gabrieli Quartet, and their own-choice recital programme stipulated that one of the pieces should be the Britten *Notturno*, re-introduced in memory of our great friend Benjamin Britten, who had died in 1976.

The finalists, who were accompanied by the BBC Northern Symphony Orchestra under Norman Del Mar, included two British competitors, Kathryn Stott and Ian Hobson, but the winner was the Frenchman Michel Dalberto, who played Mozart's

Concerto No. 25 in C. Some critics disagreed with the results as a whole, but we don't make an award on a future guess, we make it on that moment in time.

What I am against in so many critics, not only in the performing world, but in so many disciplines, is that while they may have their own opinion, if they take a dislike to someone, they can nip a beautiful talent in the bud. They have done it with some of our winners when giving their solo recitals in London. If they don't want to write anything complimentary about an established performer they will say either that they thought the person played much better earlier on, or that they are old and past it!

That was the last competition in which we were fortunate to have the guidance of Edward Boyle. Within a couple of years it became clear that he was suffering from terminal cancer. I remember a particularly poignant occasion when my pupil Ben Frith played Beethoven's great *Hammerklavier* Sonata at our house to myself, Geoffrey and Edward. After he had finished, none of us could speak – we were all overcome with emotion, as we knew that Edward was dying, and the sonata recalled Beethoven's own physical suffering from his deteriorating health – it had been written, as Beethoven himself admitted, in 'distressful circumstances'. In June 1981 Edward asked Murray Perahia if he would play the second movement of the Schubert G major Sonata at his memorial service in the University, and a couple of months later, when I went to visit him in hospital, he suggested that I should take his place as chairman of the jury in the next competition. 'This is the saddest day of my life', he said, 'but I know you will be a perfect chairman and will do the job admirably.' I realised then that Edward had finally given up hope.

But at least I was able to repay his loyalty and support. One day when Edward was already very ill, I said to Geoffrey, 'Don't you think that Edward ought to have a royal honour?' Geoffrey said, 'Well, what can you do about it?' I said, 'I can only try.' I thought of our local MP Denis Healey, a former Chancellor of the Exchequer, who we knew to be a great music-lover, and a supporter of the competition. He had often said publicly that, in his opinion, the Leeds International Piano Competition was one of the musical wonders of the world. I rang the Healeys, and Edna Healey said, 'Denis is out on his tractor at the moment, but if I tell him you're on the phone I'm sure he'll come in and have a word with you.' I said to him, 'Don't you think that Edward Boyle ought to have the highest royal honour?' He replied, 'Leave it to me. Put the phone down, and I'll speak to you later.' That was around nine o'clock in the morning. By eleven o'clock, I had a phone call from Denis, who said, 'Don't do any more about it, it is in the hands of the Prime Minister' (who was Margaret Thatcher). The upshot was that Edward was made a Companion of Honour. I rang him up, all innocence, and pretended I knew nothing about it. He told me he was very excited. As was customary, I kept my own counsel, but I thought that of all the distinguished people with whom he had come into contact, it had never occurred to anyone else, not even his former parliamentary colleagues, to suggest him as deserving of such an honour. Edward was one of the greatest human beings. He was so happy that he was made a Companion of Honour, but he never knew that I had had anything to do with it.

Edward died at the end of September 1981, aged just fifty-eight. Six months later, at a reception in St James's Palace, an appeal was launched to establish the Edward Boyle Memorial Trust, set up in his memory for the advancement of education, medicine and music. Its Patron was the Duchess of Kent, and I became one of the Trustees. We established several awards, some for medical bursaries, others to give practical and economic help to young musicians, in the form of an annual music award, to enable them to continue their studies either here or abroad. And on 6 February 1983 we organised a Gala Concert in aid of the Trust at the Royal Opera House, Covent Garden, in the presence of the Duke and Duchess of Kent. The evening was presented by Janet Baker, and performances were given by the Amadeus Quartet, Clifford Curzon, Murray Perahia, Kathryn Stott (our fifth prizewinner in 1978) and Vanya Milanova, a sensational young Bulgarian violinist who by then was married to our son Paul. I decided that such a grand occasion merited a new outfit, and unwisely remarked to Sir Harry Ognall, a local High Court Judge who was a friend of ours, that I needed a new dress as I was going to be sitting in the Royal Box at Covent Garden. After hearing my boast, Sir Harry looked at me wryly and retorted, 'As I said to the Queen yesterday, I hate name-droppers!'

The Edward Boyle Memorial Trust remained active until it was wound up in 1995, although the medical bursaries still continue.

※

EDWARD BOYLE WAS NOT THE ONLY CLOSE FRIEND we lost at that time. Both Lady Parkinson and her husband had died, also our long-serving Treasurer, Cecil Mazey, the former Vice-Chancellor of Leeds University, Sir Roger Stevens, and Charles Tapp's wife Norah. The Tapps had been faithful and generous benefactors to the competition from the very first, providing both prize-money and indispensable printing services. But for the 1981 competition we did gain some new supporters, including Arnold and Marjorie Ziff. Arnold was chairman of Stylo, a large and successful footwear group, and Marjorie a keen music-lover, so as some friends and supporters faded away, others appeared on the scene.

By 1981 we had a new Administrator, a new Treasurer, and a Publications Director in Harry Tolson, who had taken over from Charles Tapp as printer to the University of Leeds. The brochures and literature for the competition which Harry produced impressed everyone with their style, elegance and accuracy. Meanwhile I remained as Chairman and Artistic Adviser with Marion as Vice-Chairman. The past few years had been incredibly traumatic for her.

Over the years since she had married Jeremy Thorpe, rumours had begun to circulate publicly about his private life. Jeremy was being pestered by one of his alleged former lovers, and in May 1976 he was forced to resign the leadership of the Liberal Party after the publication of an incriminating letter. Three years later he and several others stood trial at the Old Bailey for incitement to murder the man who was hounding him, although the only victim had been an Alsatian dog. The prosecuting counsel was Peter Taylor QC, who later on became one of our closest friends, and Lord Chief Justice. Jeremy was defended by George Carman QC, and Marion loyally stood by him throughout the ordeal, attending court every day and facing down his accusers. The press, of course, had a field day going into all the sordid details about Jeremy's private life, which until then had been kept under cover. I used to believe that everything I read in the quality press was accurate, but in recent years my confidence in them has been severely diminished, to the point that as a joke, I say to my friends, 'When you are reading a newspaper, all you can trust is the accuracy of the date.' I thought back to my first experience of the power of a newspaper baron when I met Cecil King. The press can ruin a career in a single sentence.

Marion's friends all feared the worst, and we waited apprehensively for the result of the trial. Geoffrey and I were driving down to Windsor Castle for an evening supper party at which Rostropovich was conducting the English Chamber Orchestra, when we saw newsagents' placards with the headline: 'JEREMY THORPE ACQUITTED!' His political career, however, was over. Just before his trial began, there was a general election at which he lost the North Devon parliamentary seat he had held for twenty years. Not long after surviving this trauma he developed the first symptoms of Parkinson's disease, and Marion spent the rest of her life nursing him with stoic dedication.

%

I CHAIRED THE LEEDS JURY FOR THE FIRST TIME in the 1981 competition. One of the jurors, Claude Frank, sprang a disagreeable surprise on me on the afternoon of the second final. He announced that he wanted to go to Edinburgh to attend the wedding of his favourite nephew. 'It will be fine,' he said. 'The plane gets back to Manchester Airport fifteen minutes before the final starts.' 'Are you out of your mind?' I said. 'We all have to be in black tie, and in our places very early for the BBC.' However, I couldn't dissuade him from going – in the end he chartered a small plane, and took another four male members of the jury with him! I was terrified that there would be an accident and I might lose half my jury. But in the end, they all got back in time.

We celebrated the competition's twenty-first birthday by offering a dazzling array of prizes to the finalists including a national tour with the English Chamber Orchestra sponsored by Harveys. The rewards offered proved so enticing that for the first time in the competition's history, almost all the entrants actually turned up. There were ninety-four of them, including eleven Britons. Two of my pupils entered – Thomas Duis and Benjamin Frith – plus Ian Hobson, who had decided to have another shot after taking fourth prize in 1978, and two friends, Martin Roscoe and Peter Donohoe, who at twenty-eight was one of the oldest and most experienced entrants. Donohoe had studied music at Leeds University with Alexander Goehr. He was also a professional-level percussionist, but had decided to focus on becoming a pianist. He was already getting professional solo engagements.

Many likely candidates, including both my pupils and Martin Roscoe, were eliminated in the first round. Both Ian Hobson and Peter Donohoe reached the final and, much to his own surprise, Ian Hobson became the first British winner since Michael Roll. In retrospect, Peter Donohoe, who thought at first that the results had been read out in the wrong order, should have been placed higher than sixth. He went on the following year to win joint silver medal (no first prize being awarded) with a Russian pianist named Vladimir Ovchinnikov at the Tchaikovsky Competition. Of all the 1981 Leeds finalists, he has had by far the most successful international career, and rightly so. But one never knows at the time who is going to develop into a great artist, which Peter certainly did.

※

IN 1983 I WAS ASKED BY YORKSHIRE TELEVISION to make a series of half-hour masterclass programmes, *Fanny Waterman's*

Piano Progress, transmitted in ten parts during the autumn. The programme reproduced some of my lessons with several of my pupils, aged between eight and twenty-five, on a set designed to look like my drawing room at home. The aim was to show viewers how I related to my pupils and how I communicated my ideas to them. I have never believed in being over-polite when I am teaching, and I explained to viewers that 'I don't spare my pupils' feelings in front of the cameras, but they are used to me, and they accept my criticism.' I saw the series as a kind of musical-appreciation lesson for the general public.

Each of the half-hour programmes had a different theme, such as phrasing, rhythm and melody, how to make the piano 'sing', and what makes people listen. I felt that having pupils at different stages of development would allow me to illustrate subtle but positive points. I have always tried to spark my pupils' imagination by making interesting analogies with everyday objects, and some viewers must have been amused and intrigued to hear me likening notes to potato peelings, jewels, or grains of sugar, and comparing phrasing to darning socks! My youngest pupil was an eight-year-old virtual beginner called Sally Gorwits, and we started off with her very first lesson on the geography of the keyboard. In the last programme in the series, Sally took part in her first performance, playing a duet with my most advanced pupil, Benjamin Frith, who recorded the title music, Debussy's *Etude pour les cinq doigts*. Altogether twelve of my pupils took part in the series, but no more than three were featured in any one programme – that way we could tackle three different composers at three different levels.

SHORTLY AFTER THE YORKSHIRE TELEVISION SERIES ENDED, we began to select the entries for the next piano competition. This year, the Americans fielded an impressive list of twenty-seven candidates, and the Canadians five, including Angela Hewitt, Louis Lortie from Montreal, who won the Busoni Competition a few days before our competition opened, and Jon Kimura Parker, a student of Adele Marcus at the Juilliard School. For the first time there was also a substantial Far Eastern contingent, including nine Japanese and four Koreans. The winner was Jon Kimura Parker, who gave a stylish performance of Brahms's First Concerto. I had first heard him play at the Viña del Mar competition earlier that year, and he was so excited to have won first prize that he kissed me on both cheeks at the presentation ceremony. At the award ceremony in Leeds he kissed me again, and the Duchess of Kent, who was standing next to me, said to him, 'And may I have one too?' So Jon gave her a kiss on both cheeks. That was the first time that royal protocol had been breached so openly, in full view of a television audience of millions! It generated great publicity around the world.

When I reflect on that competition, Louis Lortie is the pianist who stands out for his wonderful artistry and poetic playing, especially in French repertoire. He took fourth prize that night, but in my opinion he was one of our greatest prizewinners. The Leeds brought him to the attention of a worldwide audience, and his career has gone from strength to strength. He is an exceptional pianist, and his recordings have won high critical acclaim.

WE WERE KEENLY AWARE that no official Russian competitors had been seen at Leeds since 1975. By the mid-1980s, there seemed to be a slight thaw in East–West relations, and the spirit of *glasnost* meant that, for the first time in many years, Russians were able to think about travelling abroad. In the summer of 1984 I was on the jury for the Santander competition in Spain. One of my fellow jurors was Lev Vlasenko, who had been on our jury in 1969. We met him again the next year in Geneva, and in 1986, when I was in Moscow as a juror at the Tchaikovsky Competition, we finally clinched a deal. Vlasenko and Tatiana Nikolaeva agreed to be on our jury for the next competition, and the Russians agreed to send some competitors.

My visit to the Tchaikovsky Competition was a memorable one. The Soviet authorities expected that their competitions would produce a Russian winner – it was a *de facto* requirement. On previous occasions when a foreign performer had done extremely well, such as John Lill in 1970, and Peter Donohoe in 1982, the jury preferred to award a joint medal with a Russian player. The one exception was the very first Tchaikovsky Competition, which had been won outright by the American Van Cliburn – no doubt to Soviet dismay, given the state of hostility between the two countries. In 1986 the Northern Irish pianist Barry Douglas was clearly ahead of the rest. As the jury went in for the final vote, Geoffrey advised me to say, as soon as we sat down, 'I propose Barry Douglas as the outright first prize-winner.' The jury voted, and he was acclaimed the winner, but the chairman of the jury was unhappy, saying that he was worried that if Barry Douglas played the Tchaikovsky around the world as well as he had just done, it would be bad for the reputation of the Russians. He proposed a re-vote. At that point I literally put my foot down. I was outraged. I banged the table with my shoe and declared that I was under the impression that we were a democratic jury, and once a vote had been taken, there should be no second vote. In the end I won the support of many other jury members, including Lev Vlasenko and Tatiana Nikolaeva, and Barry was declared the outright winner of the Gold Medal. It took some courage to challenge their system, but I triumphed. Barry has since had a fine international career. He personally selected a brand-new Steinway grand to be installed in Leeds Town Hall, which was used for the first time for the semi-finals and finals of the 1987 competition.

Fortunately I was not ostracised for my outburst on the Tchaikovsky jury, as the Russians sent three competitors to Leeds in 1987, including an eighteen-year-old student at the Moscow Conservatory called Boris Berezovsky, and twenty-nine-year-old Vladimir Ovchinnikov, who had shared the silver medal with Peter Donohoe in Moscow in 1982. Both of them reached the final. Ovchinnikov practised continuously and ferociously. Just before his final performance, in which he played Rachmaninov's Second

Concerto, the organisers couldn't get him off the practice piano. In the end Simon Rattle, who was conducting the City of Birmingham Symphony Orchestra in the finals, had to go to the practice room and persuade Ovchinnikov to join him on the platform, saying, 'Come on, we can do it together!' Ovchinnikov was declared the winner, with Berezovsky in fourth place.

15

THOUGHTS ON COMPETITIONS

Competition is part of life. In the foreword to the brochure of our very first Leeds Competition, I wrote:

> We believe it is of the utmost importance for young artists to have the opportunity of hearing their musical contemporaries in an atmosphere of friendly rivalry, and we hope that the Leeds International Pianoforte Competition will provide a forum for competition of a truly 'Olympic' standard.

Musical competitions have taken place for thousands of years. In Greek myth, the god of music, Apollo, challenged the satyr Marsyas to a trial of skill. The judges were Apollo's daughters, the Nine Muses, who almost inevitably decided in favour of their father. There was no prize for winning, but the loser was flayed alive for his temerity in challenging the god. We certainly don't inflict that fate on our less successful competitors, but all of us – especially the jury – do tend to get flayed by the judgements of the critics.

Music was almost certainly included, alongside sport, in the 'Olympic' contests of ancient Greece, and the public comparison of song performances played a major part in the activities of the medieval *Meistersinger* and *Minnesinger* guilds, and among French *trouvères*. Several of the most famous composers submitted themselves to public tests of skill. When J. S. Bach visited Dresden in the autumn of 1717, he challenged the visiting French organist and composer Louis Marchand to an improvisation contest on the keyboard. When the time came for the contest, Bach and the judges waited anxiously for the opponent, but in vain. Eventually they discovered that Marchand had left Dresden by the dawn mail-coach, evidently fearing to test his skill against such a 'skilful and galant' opponent. And a decade earlier, the young Handel submitted himself to a keyboard-playing contest against Domenico Scarlatti. Scarlatti was declared the better harpsichordist, but Handel a far better organist.

Another famous musical competition between keyboard players was staged by the Austrian Emperor Josef II on Christmas Eve 1781, when Mozart and Clementi were asked to improvise variations and fugues for the entertainment of the court. Mozart won the composing element, but Clementi was declared the superior in terms of showmanship. The Emperor couldn't decide between them, and declared the duel a draw. Clementi was most complimentary about Mozart's playing, declaring that, until then, he had never heard anyone play with such spirit and grace. Mozart, however, was less gracious. He wrote to his father, 'Clementi plays well, as far as execution with the right hand goes. His greatest strength lies in his passages in thirds. Apart from that, he has not a kreuzer's worth of taste or feeling – in short, he is a mere technician.' Over fifty years later, yet another contest between two of the greatest pianists of their day – Liszt and Thalberg – also ended in a draw.

Unfortunately, we can't have 'draws' at the Leeds. It is in the competition's rules that a first prize must be awarded. It would look very bad if a competition of the standard and prestige of Leeds, which attracts the cream of young players, failed to produce a clear first prize-winner who stands a good chance of making a career. And it would be very difficult to persuade the donors of engagements to fulfil their obligations. We have a duty to the competitors to say to someone, 'You were first past the post. We're opening doors for you and giving you marvellous opportunities. Your future success is now up to you.'

Young winners in local competitions are all too often showered with praise by relatives and friends who tell them that they are geniuses, when in reality they are not geniuses, but highly gifted children. They may have a string of successes in local competitions, and become big fishes in little ponds. The next 'test' for dedicated and determined competitors is to try their luck in a national competition, with the advice of their teachers. The air is much rarer here, they are expected to reach a much higher standard of playing, and they often have to give a recital to include masterpieces by the great composers, as well as pieces of their own choice.

One vital quality that is essential for success in an international competition is stamina. At a competition such as the Leeds, a competitor faces three solo rounds of thirty, fifty-five and seventy-five minutes respectively – all from memory, before the final concerto round with orchestra. Some competitions, as the Leeds did for several years, also include a chamber-music round. Many major competitions are extremely selective in their pre-selection of candidates, limiting the starters to some 35 or 40, whereas we have always believed that you have to have a lot of milk to produce a little cream, so we start with around 70, and give them thirty minutes each in the first stage.

The career of a solo pianist is the loneliest in the world. It takes real grit. You are always on trial: if you make a mistake it will instantly be criticised, and you have to face those hostile reviews. Life is especially tough for competition winners. Many critics have a preconceived idea that you may have a good technique, but no originality. You have to take into account the past, the present, and the future. The past is the foundation on which you have built your technique and your approach to the study of music. The present requires nerves of steel – the ability to walk on to the platform and forget all the technical groundwork – what you have to be able to do is to find the inspiration to produce the magic that makes people listen. And you are only ever as good as your last performance. A few mediocre performances can easily cancel out the memory of past good ones. It's not a glamorous life. The strain of a competition is some kind of preparation for that life – but in some ways it's a different situation. When a competitor comes on to the platform, everybody – the jury, the organisers, the audience – wants him or her to play well.

Can a young pianist become a great artist without winning a competition? You must be very lucky indeed to make it to the top through other routes – perhaps Lang Lang and Benjamin Grosvenor are the most obvious examples today. But look at Radu Lupu – he'd already won the Van Cliburn, but it didn't give him the kind of career he wanted. So he had the courage to enter at Leeds. And Murray Perahia had already played with the New York Philharmonic. He came to England shortly before the Leeds competition and tried to get one of the London agents to take him on. But they weren't interested, not until after he won the Leeds. The engagements offered to each of those artists as a result of winning at Leeds gave them the opportunity to reveal their qualities. It gives the winners a chance.

I live with the criticism that competitions can do more harm than good. I disagree with this point of view. There is always competition – in life, as in any field of artistic endeavour. The career of a concert artist begins the day after you win a major competition. You are plunged into the ocean, and you have to swim very hard to keep afloat, and to reach for the lifebelts that professional engagements represent. Only after winning a prize at a major international competition does the competition of real life start – from now on the winners are compared to all the great pianists of the past and present, irrespective of age and nationality, and not only to pianists of their own generation.

I would ask, 'What are the alternatives to competitions?' In the bad old days, the usual route was through privilege, money or influence. Sometimes an impresario would take up an artist, but it was all very hit and miss. Today the cost of putting on a recital in London as a self-promotion, advertising and playing (often to a tiny handful of friends and relatives) is almost prohibitive, and there is absolutely no guarantee that an audience or any influential critics will turn up. And if critics do come, their knives may well be sharpened and they may nip a beautiful talent in the bud. But this is only one man's opinion! Dame Janet Baker says that if you want to be a success in the music world, you must learn to run a business as well as being an outstanding performer.

Does the best person always win? So far as the Leeds International Piano Competition is concerned, the jury, having listened to around a hundred solo recitals and six concertos in nearly three weeks arrives at the conclusion that *this* competitor at *this* time and in *this* place shall be proclaimed the winner. However, anything might happen in the future, and the jury has no access to a crystal ball. There is no means of guessing how successful competitors may react to future fortunes and misfortunes. They are entering competitions at the time in their lives when they might fall in love, marry, may separate and divorce. Such emotional traumas may play havoc with their professional lives as musicians. We, as a jury, do not know if the winner possesses the necessary reserves of physical and emotional stamina to deal with such traumas. Nor do we know how they might react to adverse criticism in the press – will they be able to shrug it off and keep going? We cannot know how they deal with nerves, which are inevitable, and which often affect the standard of individual performances. Nor can we tell how much intensive teaching went into the preparation of the competition programmes, and whether the winner might be overly dependent on his or her teacher. Nor do we know how they will cope with jetlag and incessant travelling, being away from friends and family, while at the same time absorbing and memorising new repertoire.

Only time will tell. But what we do know is that, at Leeds, the audience wants the competitors to play well, the jury wants to hear them play well – even the critics come here hoping to hear them play well. They will never find that goodwill again. Out there the critics will be waiting to devour them unless they are a really great talent. After Leeds, that's when the competition of real life starts.

Winning an international competition opens many doors. We can only hope that these doors will remain open for the rest of their lives.

16

BEFORE AND BEYOND
THE MILLENNIUM

*Music is therapeutic. It rejoices with us in our successes. It encourages
us in our disappointments and consoles us in times of sorrow.*
FANNY WATERMAN

By 1990 we had extended the duration of the Leeds International
Piano Competition by three days, in order to allow each competitor to play for forty minutes rather than twenty in the first
round. I felt that if more time was allocated, it would give each
competitor time to settle down and to show off the architecture
of a major work. Twenty-five competitors rather than twenty
would be admitted to the second round, and there would be
twelve, rather than ten, semi-finalists. We also dropped the
chamber-music round. Own-choice pieces were introduced as well
as a prescribed piece in the first round, as we felt that any professional pianist should be able to demonstrate the ability to
construct a good recital programme.

The biggest upset of the 1990 competition occurred in the
semi-final round. One of the most promising competitors was
Piotr Anderszewski, a young Pole who had won the 1987
National Chopin Competition. His recital programme consisted
of just two works – Beethoven's huge *Diabelli* Variations, and
Webern's tiny, three-movement Op. 27 Variations. Having
delivered a magisterial exposition of the Beethoven, he returned
for the Webern, only to seem to freeze up just before the third
and last variation. He rose from the piano stool and left the platform. It was a shock, but Anderszewski's career has not suffered

at all. He has since proved himself a truly remarkable pianist – one of the greats.

Even without Anderszewski, the 1990 competition uncovered some major talents, including Karl-Heinz Kämmerling's pupil Lars Vogt and twenty-five-year-old Eric Le Sage from France, who had won first prize in the 1989 Schumann Competition. All but two of the competitors that year, but not the eventual winner, Artur Pizarro from Portugal, who played Rachmaninov's Third Concerto, played the Schumann, and Simon Rattle and the CBSO pulled off the near-miraculous feat of accompanying four very different interpretations of the same piece.

The American critic Harold Schonberg, who was on the jury, said he thought the 1990 Leeds competition was the strongest he had ever judged, and he would have been satisfied giving first prize to any of the first three finalists. Our runner-up Lars Vogt in particular has had a very successful career, both as pianist and conductor. He has escalated his playing to new heights, has just been appointed Music Director of the Royal Northern Sinfonia at the Sage in Gateshead from the 2015–16 season and is a favourite of the BBC.

※

IN 1993 GEOFFREY, HAVING REACHED HIS SEVENTIETH BIRTHDAY, decided to retire after forty-three years at the GP practice in Morley. The colleague who succeeded him as Senior Partner, on his own retirement in 2014, paid tribute to Geoffrey, saying he had been greatly respected as a physician and as a man of great intellect and wisdom, who had been genuinely committed to his patients. On Geoffrey's sixty-fifth birthday, one of his patients had written a charming poem about him, which we framed and hung on the wall:

> *Dear Doctor de Keyser*
> *It's your birthday today,*
> *So just sit down quietly,*
> *I've a few words to say.*

You're as much a part of Morley,
As the seven well-known hills,
For many long years now,
You've helped cure our chills.

You arrived as a young chap,
With dashing good looks,
All the young Morley ladies
Queued to get on your books.

Oh! Isn't he handsome!
Have you heard his deep voice?
And how many doctors
Have had a Rolls-Royce?

You settled in quickly,
Midst the mills and the muck,
And got by on judgement,
Not merely by luck.

One thing that confused folk
Was your strange-sounding name,
De-Kyper? Dick Eyser?
Well it sounds just the same.

Your surgery in Queen Street
Was cosy but dark,
And the cigs that you smoked then
Made you splutter and bark.

Remember those bottles,
That sat on your shelf,
For the potions and medicines
You made up yourself.

'Doc, give me that red stuff,
Cos the green just won't work,
Yes, I've really got back-ache,
And I'm not trying to shirk!'

Though years have rolled on now,
You're still well respected,
You've got a few wrinkles,
But don't feel dejected.

You may pull odd faces,
And peer over your specs,
But you're still greatly admired
By the opposite sex.

So being sixty-five
Is not bad at all,
Just count all your blessings,
With love from us all.

After retirement, Geoffrey had more time to devote to the administrative side of the competition at home, and also to accompanying me on my overseas visits as a jury member. His wisdom, eloquent speech, engaging personality and authoritative musical knowledge enhanced the prestige of the competition wherever we went.

The disintegration of the former Soviet Union four years earlier meant that opportunities were now opening up for pianists from the former Eastern Bloc countries. Before then, only three pianists were allowed to represent the Soviet Union in any one competition. In 1993 the largest contingent for our competition came from the former Soviet Union, and two Russians reached the final. The overall winner, however, was the Brazilian Ricardo Castro, with Britain's Leon McCawley, who had just taken first prize at the Vienna Beethoven Competition, coming a close second.

That was the last year in which the prizes were presented by our Patron, HRH The Duchess of Kent, who in her capacity as Chancellor of the University of Leeds, also conferred a doctorate in music on Simon Rattle during the presentation ceremony. I myself had been awarded an honorary doctorate by the University of Leeds in 1992. In July 1995 I was honoured with a further doctorate from the University of York, of which Dame Janet Baker, who was to become the new Patron of our competition in 2000 following the Duchess of Kent's retirement, was the Chancellor. This is an extract from the speech I gave on that occasion:

> Chancellor, Vice-Chancellor, Fellow Graduates, Ladies and Gentlemen –
>
> I feel particularly gratified to be welcomed by this seat of learning because, of all professions, I regard teaching as the most important. One cannot become a singer, doctor, lawyer, engineer, chef or joiner without guidance, and everyone here today is aware of the tremendous inspiration and influences that teachers have had over us, from our earliest days. This chain of influence is infinite.
>
> This has been a wonderful day of achievement for us all and a milestone in our lives. You needed, in addition to your own ability and experienced guidance from your teachers, determination, concentration, application and inspiration; and very often there will have been frustration, tribulation, and, I am sure, always perspiration.
>
> Most of these qualities are present in every walk of life and there is no short cut to education and learning in any sphere. There is a tripartite aspect to the rhythm of life, connecting the past, present and future because everything which happens in the present (such as your achievement today) is related to your endeavours in the past and will influence your future. There is no dividing line between these time zones, only a seamless continuum – the joins are undetectable.

If I may speak to each one of you personally for a moment – as a musician – I would like to emphasise the power and importance of music in our lives. It touches all our hearts, enriches our lives and follows us from the cradle to the grave. Music can portray every mood and emotion, as in the slow movement of the Funeral March Sonata of Chopin, the joy and grandeur of Handel's 'Hallelujah' Chorus, the melting tenderness of a Schubert song, or the wit and sparkle of a Mendelssohn scherzo.

All of you here today could become music-lovers by listening to the great musical masterpieces with humility, and preferably attending live performances . . . I could make a case for considering that the study of Music, together with that of an instrument to a reasonable degree of proficiency, is a discipline which can equip a person for many valuable walks of life. I, personally, have had piano students that illustrate this well. One of whom, a girl, became a managing executive at Rolls-Royce Aero Engines manufacture and was accepted by British Airways on to their transatlantic pilots' training scheme. The managing director wrote to me asking for a reference regarding her application. I replied, saying 'If she can respond to the discipline, diligence and demands required by my lessons, then she will respond well in any emergency situation.' Another such pupil of mine, a young man, has recently become a High Court Judge. And of course, there is always the example of Sir Edward Heath, who read Music and became prime minister.

I know that our Chancellor has devoted her life to music – *die holde Kunst*. She has been an inspiration and an example for us all to follow.

This has been one of the happiest days in my life as, I am sure, it has been for everyone here in this Congregation. Your teachers, proud parents and friends wish you well for all your future endeavours.

℁

IN 1994 I MADE MY FIRST APPEARANCE on a Chinese jury at the inaugural International Chinese Piano Competition in Beijing. Interest in piano playing was soaring in China and the Far East and, from now on, the Leeds would attract an increasing number of competitors from China, Japan and Korea. After the 1993 competition I visited Japan at the invitation of the Tokyu Bunkamura Foundation. Bunkamura is the Japanese for 'cultural village', and Tokyu, a business conglomerate built on shipping and retail, had had endowed a huge arts complex in the Shibuya district of Tokyo. By then we knew that Harveys was withdrawing its sponsorship of the Leeds, and I mentioned that we were looking for alternative sources of sponsorship. Almost immediately Bunkamura said they were interested. Our association with them enabled us to raise the prize money for the 1996 competition, and in addition the winner was offered a lucrative Japanese concert tour paid for by the Bunkamura Foundation. Altogether, around ninety national and international engagements would be available to the prizewinners, together with a recording prize offered by Naxos for each of two finalists.

In May 1998 Leeds Town Hall was to close for renovations, re-opening in spring 2000 as part of the Millennium celebrations. That meant it would be out of action in 1999, when the next competition was due to take place. More importantly, Simon Rattle (now Sir Simon) told us that he would not be available for the 1999 final as he would be conducting in Vienna. So we made the decision that for the first time in the competition's history, there would be a four-year gap between competitions, and the thirteenth competition would take place in Millennium Year.

※

I CELEBRATED MY EIGHTIETH BIRTHDAY IN MARCH 2000. Two months later I was honoured and delighted to be awarded the CBE in the Queen's Birthday Honours List, and Geoffrey and I went to the Palace with our sons to collect the award. Looking back, it was a joyful but poignant occasion. We were deeply worried about Geoffrey's health. For over a year he had been suffering from a kidney complaint. He went for X-rays, and as soon as he was shown them he just said one word: 'carcinoma'. From that moment, our lives changed completely. Our world fell apart, and a dark shadow descended, as we realised that never again would we be able to enjoy carefree parties or musical evenings. At first we went through a period of non-acceptance – life had taken on a sense of unreality, and instead of waking up each morning full of the joys of life, I felt weighed down by a feeling of dread and apprehension. As a doctor himself, Geoffrey was aware of the disease and its progression, and it was very hard to carry on with some kind of normal life. Geoffrey insisted that I should continue to attend every meeting of the competition's committee throughout the course of his illness, and I have never missed a meeting in fifty years, even in the week leading up to his death.

My deep anxiety about Geoffrey overshadowed preparations for the thirteenth competition, held in September 2000, but our dedication to the competition and its continued success never wavered. It was the last of four in which the finals were accompanied by the CBSO under Sir Simon Rattle, who was about to leave the UK to take up his new post as Chief Conductor of the Berlin Philharmonic Orchestra. I am overjoyed with his recent announcement that he will return to the UK in 2017 to take the helm at the London Symphony Orchestra. Sir Simon is an incalculable asset to the musical life of this country and the world, and a powerful ambassador for music and music education. Since Sir Simon's departure in 2003, the Leeds finals have been accompanied by the Hallé Orchestra conducted by Sir Mark Elder. He is a marvellous communicator and educator of audiences, and is a star in his own right.

Three nationalities seem to have dominated the Leeds over the first decade of the twenty-first century – Italians, Russians and Asians, particularly from China and Korea. The rise of exceptional pianists trained in Italy seems to be associated with the important International Piano Academy at Imola, where guest lecturers have included many pianists – both former jurors and competitors associated with Leeds. I myself have also given masterclasses there. The regular teaching staff includes some excellent professors, among them Boris Petrushansky, one of our 1969 finalists. Petrushansky's brilliant students include our 2009 and 2012 winners, Sofya Gulyak and Federico Colli, and I have invited him to be a member of the 2015 Leeds jury.

After the 2000 competition, I left for jury duty in China, accompanied by Geoffrey. We probably should not have gone, as by that time he was in considerable distress. He went downhill very quickly, and I went downhill with him. We were united in our moods. One day we would feel more optimistic, only to have our hopes dashed when a further medical investigation proved that the growth was not responding to treatment. I can only compare our feelings to that of a pianist waiting to mount the platform steps in a competition, waiting in trepidation to take that lonely walk under the spotlight to a black piano. But this was a matter of life or death. We were teetering on the edge of a precipice – neither of us knew how long it would be before the inevitable happened.

In the early summer of 2001 the Incorporated Society of Musicians bestowed its Distinguished Musician Award on me. The ceremony was held at the Royal College of Music. During the dinner, Geoffrey left the table and was away for a long time. When he finally came back, he said, 'I have to go to a hospital.' He was taken away in an ambulance, and later transferred to hospital in Leeds. My German friend Karin, who had looked after my family when they were younger, came to help and comfort me. Geoffrey passed away in July. All his former colleagues at the medical practice, as well as the many people who knew him from our work on the competition, paid tribute to him. Simon Rattle wrote to me, 'Your marriage was made in heaven, and you were successful when so many of us have failed.'

I was distraught and disorientated. During fifty-seven years of marriage, he had been my rock and my inspiration. Eventually I pulled myself together enough to accept a dinner invitation from a life-long friend called Iris Haller, who has just celebrated her own centenary, which somehow gave me hope. And from that low point, I began the long climb back from those dark days of grieving.

※

BY 2003 THE BUDGET FOR THE Leeds International Piano Competition had risen to over half a million pounds. We were offering the winners a hundred recital and concerto engagements in the UK, Europe, North America and the Far East.

We had twelve Russian entrants that year, and only four from the UK. The finalists came from Asia, Uzbekistan, Ukraine and the UK, but the winner was Antii Siirala from Finland. At the prize-giving ceremony, Dame Janet Baker, our new Patron, told the competitors, 'You will never play to a more knowledgeable audience, a more intelligent audience, or a more generous audience.'

After Geoffrey died, I had no one with whom to talk about music, and felt isolated as a result. Dame Janet came to my rescue, and has become my confidante, 'a very present help in trouble', as the Bible says, and a firm supporter of the competition. She is one of the finest artists of our time: her velvety contralto voice, her peerless interpretations and her sense of humanity have made her beloved of audiences all over the world, as well as of individuals such as myself who have benefited from her wisdom and selfless generosity of spirit.

Of all the great artists I have met, Dame Janet stands out. She has had a profound influence on my own musicianship and my musical life. She herself has described music as a 'fourth dimension, containing within it the elements of past, present, and future'. Hearing her sing has made me realise that the human voice is the most beautiful of all instruments. We have sat together on juries of other international competitions, and developed a mutual respect for each other as colleagues and friends. After her retirement from singing, she remained only as Chancellor of York University and as Patron of the Leeds International Piano Competition. I invited her to be our Patron because of her great knowledge and deep love of music, and she has told me that she will remain as Patron for the competition's Golden Jubilee, but will stay only so long as I am still Chairman and Artistic Director – 'When you retire, I go,' she said. Her husband, Keith Shelley, gave up a career in banking to manage her career, and now that he is gravely ill and needs her, she has given up everything to look after him. I have treasured all the letters that Dame Janet has written me. When we speak together, we talk as intimates. She understands my difficulties, when I feel that I am surrounded by musical upstarts, and consoles me if I am distressed. She says she always looks forward to my calls, which often begin, 'Janet, I have some very exciting news to tell you ...' It has been one of the greatest privileges of my life to count her as a friend.

※

LOOKING BACK OVER THE PAST FIFTEEN YEARS, I am struck by the inexorable rise of young Asian pianists, both in number and quality. There has certainly been an explosion of pianistic talent in the Far East. It reflects the immense dedication shown by young aspiring pianists there, who start learning the piano very young, often at around the age of four. Their early lessons provide them with a strong foundation for future success. I've visited conservatories in China where there are children under the age of ten who can already play several concertos. They have marvellous teachers who have themselves been given scholarships to study in Europe, Britain, or America, where they imbibe Western culture, and then they go back to teach in their own countries. Asian parents are wonderfully supportive of their children. They are dedicated and devoted. Many of my own pupils now come from the Far East.

In 2006 our prize-winner's engagements included a tour of China, and of the seventy-one first-round pianists, thirty-three came from Asian countries, or were of Asian extraction. Four reached the finals, including two very fine pianists and musicians, the Koreans, Kim Sung-Hoon and eighteen-year-old Sunwook Kim. I first heard Sunwook at the 2005 Clara Haskil Competition in Geneva. After he had won it, we shared a taxi, and I suggested he should enter the Leeds and stop smoking! Nothing ruffles this remarkable young pianist. He remained unperturbed throughout his second-round recital at Leeds, which was disrupted by rain dripping through the roof of the University's Great Hall. In the final, in which he played Brahms's First Piano Concerto, a member of the audience fainted noisily and had to be carried out, but he simply continued. He was declared the winner – the youngest since Michael Roll – and is without doubt one of our finest recent laureates. He has said, 'My childhood dreams – winning first place at competitions or signing contracts – have all come true at a relatively early age. It's true that I've worked hard to achieve them, and I just want to keep it up.' He will carry the banner of our competition into every concert hall throughout the world.

The year 2006 was certainly the 'Year of the Piano' in Leeds. The BBC organised an event called 'Pianos Everywhere' to coincide with the competition's final weekend. Instruments were installed in unusual locations all around the city, including the Chinatown Shopping Arcade, Kirkgate Market, Leeds City Station and the Queens Hotel, encouraging members of the public to sit down and play them. The Lord Mayor started proceedings by playing *Chopsticks* in the entrance to Waitrose! Ben Frith gave a special performance, and together with the other members of the Gould Trio, organised musical workshops for pupils from two primary schools in Chapeltown. It really was a Big Piano Party. I thought it was a wonderful idea, to bring the piano and piano music to a wider audience. As I have found throughout my life, the piano can bring so much enjoyment to so many people. Leeds rang with piano music that weekend, and the event was a perfect complement to our competition.

Three years later China provided the largest contingent of competitors, including two aged just fourteen and sixteen. The sheer industry and application of these Chinese students is astonishing. Nevertheless, while the winner of the 2009 competition provided a 'first' for Leeds, it was as a result of gender, not nationality. We have had some superb women pianists in our list of prizewinners, from Viktoria Postnikova to Mitsuko Uchida, but no woman had ever won the first prize. The Gold Medal and the £15,000 First Prize went to a twenty-nine-year-old Russian, Sofya Gulyak, who had studied with Boris Petrushansky in Imola. Sofya said that she regarded her gender as irrelevant – it was winning that mattered to her, not the fact that she was the first female winner.

※

BY 2012 ALMOST FIFTY YEARS had elapsed since Marion and I founded the Leeds International Piano Competition. In that year, introduced by Sir David Tang (a great connoisseur of music), the Chinese pianist Lang Lang became our Global Ambassador. He sent a message, saying:

> To the pianists' mother, Dame Fanny,
> I am a pianist performing throughout the world, and I don't think there has been a concert hall around the globe that has not felt the impact of The Leeds International Piano Competition in the great names it has helped on their way. I am truly honoured to be associated with this tradition, and I can only say that your vision will live on as a positive force for many years to come.
> Thanks for the inspiration to all of us.

We were also delighted to appoint as our Honorary Ambassador Daw Aung San Suu Kyi, who visited Britain in 2012 for the first time after her long and cruel period of internment in her native country. Deprived of her husband and children, and confined under solitary house arrest, she had spent many hours playing the piano, which was her only solace. She also heard all the Leeds International Piano Competition broadcasts on the BBC World Service. During her visit she was entertained by the prime minister, and said she would particularly like to meet me. The prime minister had to think of a suitable parting gift which would remind this remarkable and courageous woman of her visit to England, and it was suggested that it would be most appropriate if the Leeds International Piano Competition were to award its prestigious Winner's Gold Medal in her name. She was absolutely delighted. It is hoped that Sir David Tang and I will pay a return visit shortly.

As always, the competition received financial support from Leeds City Council, and the practical support of the University. Without a major single sponsor, we relied on a growing list of help from private trusts and foundations, commercial companies and generous individual benefactors. The prize fund – donated by a variety of individuals and charitable trusts including the Linden Charitable Trust, the Liz and Terry Bramall Charitable Trust, the Marjorie and Arnold Ziff Charitable Foundation, David Goldman, Anita Woolman, Dr Keith Howard, the Burton family, Lady Solti (in memory of her husband and parents), and Robert Tebb – now offered a first prize of £18,000 as well as the Gold Medal, and a debut solo CD recording offered by Champs Hill records. Second to sixth prizes this year ranged from £12,000 to £3,500. In addition to the semi-final prizes of £1500, the businessman Sir David Tang offered a unique Audience Prize of £200 at each of the first three stages of the competition – to go to the audience member who most closely matched the jury's votes. In addition we introduced a new award. The Hallé Orchestra donated the Terence Judd–Hallé Orchestra prize of £5000 plus at least three paid engagements with the orchestra and a concert at the Bridgewater Hall. This prize, awarded to a finalist nominated by the members of the orchestra, aimed to perpetuate Terence's memory.

The BBC, who has been our official broadcast partners since 2009, did us proud in 2012. BBC4 television produced a six-week series of programmes featuring the six finalists and their concerto performances in full, taking viewers behind the scenes at 'The Leeds'. On Radio 3 the coverage of the competition introduced a six-week series of programmes featuring the piano, in which some of our past laureates – Perahia, Lupu, Pizarro, Schiff, Uchida, Vogt and Lortie – took part.

Although entrants from Far Eastern countries are beginning to dominate the Leeds in terms of numbers, they are not as yet sweeping the board in terms of prizes. The 2012 finalists reflected an interesting spread of nationalities. Only one, Jiayan Sun, was Chinese. The others were Jayson Gillham from Australia, Andrew Tyson from the USA, Andrejs Osokins from Latvia, Federico Colli from Italy and Louis Schwizgebel from Switzerland. The final was of a tremendously high standard, and it was a tense, close-fought contest. We had a very difficult decision as jury members, particularly having to choose between two exciting Beethoven performances – Colli's majestic *Emperor*, and Schwizgebel's poetic account of the Fourth. In the end, the first prize went to Colli, with Schwizgebel as runner-up. Both are outstanding pianists, and we look forward to their future careers. The Orchestra Prize and fifth place went to Andrew Tyson, who certainly had the conductor and orchestra behind him. Andrew has since returned to Leeds to give recitals in aid of the competition.

I was touched that after thirty-one years, a rift was finally healed when Peter Donohoe visited the competition and we engaged in a public 'conversazione'. Peter felt that the Leeds had not treated him well in 1981, but he has written that in time he came to appreciate that neither his career nor his public profile has suffered in the long term by his association with the competition, in fact, the reverse is true. For my own part, I consider him one of the best British pianists of our time, and I greatly admire his playing.

17

FAMILY AND FRIENDS

People live on the other side of the mountain too. Be modest! You
never thought of or invented anything that others had not thought
of or invented before you. And even if you had done so, you should
consider it a gift from heaven, which you should share with others.

ROBERT SCHUMANN

At the mid-point of my tenth decade, I often reflect on the three
Ages of Life: Youth, Middle Age, and How Well You Look.

As I sit in my kitchen, watching the squirrels running up and
down the wooden bird-feeder outside the window, I'm thinking
back to an incident in my childhood when I screamed for a pair
of dainty ankle-strap shoes that I really wanted so much. I cried
all the way home! I can hear my father saying irritably in Yiddish,
'Does she REALLY need them?" and my mother replying:
'Definitely NOT!' Buying them was such a struggle for my parents
at the time. Now, ninety years later, I could easily afford them,
but I no longer have the feet to wear them as I have a bunion. They
lie in a shoe box, shrouded in white tissue paper, never again to
see the light of day. I used to love dancing as a child.

It's the small things in life that make you truly happy. I love the
way the seasons slip seamlessly from daffodils and snowdrops in
spring to perfumed, coloured roses in summer, the russet and
golden colours of autumn, and powdery white snowflakes in
winter. I love sunset and dawn, birdsong in spring, the full moon,
the sound of waves on a shore or rain lashing at a window, and the
magical appearance of a rainbow. I love the smell of fresh coffee

and fresh bread, a purring kettle, and the human voice in song. I love the first glimpse of a newborn baby, and the sound of laughing children at play.

All these things were important to me when I was young, and I still love them now. In middle age, I reached a benchmark in my life, when my early desires and hopes for a career in music began to come true, and my gift for music enabled me to make a significant difference to many people.

My father always told me, 'My good lass, be thankful you have the work and the strength to do it.' He continued to drive his car well into his nineties, and I have as much energy now as I did in my twenties. 'If you don't use it, you lose it,' he said. I am still flattered when someone says, 'How well you look!' It's not simply one's appearance, it is a spiritual *joie de vivre* which shows that I am still optimistic for the future. I am surrounded by loving friends, children, grandchildren and great-grandchildren, as well as former and present pupils and their parents, who demonstrate a warmth and appreciation of what I have tried to do and have actually achieved.

I learnt so much from my parents: always to respect people but not possessions that money can buy, to value good health, talent, beauty, reliability, generosity and integrity.

These days I feel that many young people are growing up with the wrong values. They have a lack of respect for their elders. As the Bible says, 'Honour thy father and thy mother, that their days may be long upon the earth.' I was so glad that my parents both lived to see me fulfil many of their dreams and aspirations, and they were so proud when I was awarded an OBE for services to music in 1971. I wish they could have been there when their daughter, the child of poor Russian immigrants, was granted the Freedom of the City of Leeds in April 2004 in 'recognition and high appreciation of her outstanding contribution to music and music teaching, internationally, and for her extraordinary commitment to the Leeds International Piano Competition', and was made a Dame Commander of the British Empire in the 2005 New Year Honours List. It is one of my greatest sorrows that

Geoffrey was not at my side when I went to the Palace to receive the honour. Instead, my sons supported me, and my family has been a source of great joy.

Both Robert and Paul attended Leeds Grammar School, and both of them opted to learn the violin, rather than the piano. They had heard my highly gifted pupils, and I couldn't get them to learn their scales. So I sent them to the Leeds violin teacher Eta Cohen instead. Lesson: never teach your wife or husband to drive a car, or your children to learn a musical instrument! The boys both played in the National Youth Orchestra. When Robert left school he went on to Leeds University, where he took a BSc in Bio-chemistry and Physiology in 1974. Four years later he qualified as a chartered accountant after training with Price Waterhouse, but since 1980 he has worked in the fashion trade, running his own business as an independent international distributor for major brands. He has five daughters, Alexandra, Gemma, Lara, Tasha and Rosie. In August 2014 his daughter Gemma gave him his first grandchild, Sebastian, and in June 2015 Alex also gave birth to a baby boy, Zachary.

Paul gained his ARCM Performers' Diploma with Honours at the age of only sixteen, becoming the youngest person ever to achieve that. He went on to study at the Guildhall School of Music and Drama with Yfrah Neaman, and became a highly respected violin teacher. He followed my example by publishing a successful series of violin tutors with Faber Music. There are now fifteen books in the series, which is sold all over the world. In 1978 Paul married the violinist Vanya Milanova, whom he met at the Guildhall. They have a daughter, Carmella, who is also now married with a son, Leart. So in addition to six granddaughters, I now have three great-grandsons. The births of these grandchildren and great-grandchildren feel like the most wonderful gift. I treasure a letter that Carmella sent me last year:

Dearest Grandma
  You have achieved things which most families take generations to develop, yet you managed to accomplish them

in one lifetime! We are REALLY proud of you and want you to remember that once was, always is!

All our love and kisses,
CARMELLA, ERION and LEART

My brother Harry worked as a solicitor in Leeds throughout his life, until his untimely death in 1973. Harry inherited my father's left-wing views. He was a member of the Fabian Society, and stood for Parliament as a Labour candidate in the February 1956 by-election, and again at the 1959 general election, but his Conservative opponent Sir Keith Joseph won the seat. His three children are all musical, and David is the cellist with the Endellion Quartet.

The Georgian statesman Lord Chesterfield said that one must travel through the world one's self to be acquainted with it, and I look back with pleasure on some memorable family holidays, often with musical associations. When the boys were quite young we visited Pörtschach on the Wörthersee in Carinthia, where Brahms spent his summer holidays and wrote his Second Symphony, the Violin Concerto and the Second Violin Sonata, and Bad Gastein, which was one of Schubert's favourite summer haunts. We also visited Mozart's birthplace in Salzburg; the Villa d'Este on Lake Como, whose fountains inspired Liszt's great piano piece; and the monastery of Valdemossa on Majorca, where Chopin composed some of his Preludes, including the 'Raindrop'. When my younger son Paul took a gap year between school and university in the mid-1970s, he and I visited my aunt Bessie's son Ronnie in Sydney, and went on to Hong Kong and Tokyo, where I gave a masterclass. We also visited Israel, where I had been invited to be a guest of honour at the first Rubinstein Competition. On Paul's eighteenth birthday we were in New York, where we stayed in a Fifth Avenue apartment belonging to the Moskovitzes, overlooking Central Park and the Metropolitan Museum. It felt incredibly glamorous.

I love my home, a fine, solid, Victorian house in a quiet road on the southern edge of Roundhay Park, of which I had many happy childhood memories. Geoffrey and I moved there in 1966, and it has been our family home ever since. It has a large back garden, where first our boys, and later on our grandchildren, could play, and an elegant drawing room where over the years we have entertained many of the distinguished musicians who visited Leeds for the competition. Geoffrey bought me the first of two beautiful Steinway grand pianos after we moved there, for our twenty-fifth wedding anniversary in 1969. Alfred Brendel and Clifford Curzon helped me choose it. We bought the other while I was doing the *Piano Progress* masterclasses. The two pianos sit side by side in my drawing room, and they have been my constant companions ever since.

I think the worst words in the English language are 'I can't be bothered' – one must always make time for other people. Life should be full of reciprocity and giving time and happiness to other people makes me happy. The world is full of givers and takers, and I feel I been a giver all my life. I don't like cynical or sarcastic people, who like to have fun at other people's expense. I prefer to live my life according to Lord Chesterfield's advice to his son: 'An able man [or woman] shows his spirit by gentle words and resolute actions.'

Sometimes, in the course of my work in music education when I have been visiting some of the poorest schools in Leeds, the pupils have said to me, 'What is it like, being famous?' and I reply, 'That's a very difficult question to answer. It's not something you think about, it becomes part of your subconscious. It's not an objective in itself, but it does become a challenge. When you are given a little job, you must do it to the best of your ability, and then someone notices and gives you a bigger job, and so it goes on.'

After Geoffrey passed away my musical career saved me. My students and my musical friends have kept me from feeling lonely, and the sincere love of genuine friends, such as Dame Janet Baker, who lifts my spirits and is a great support in difficult times. Since my early days, I have found that choosing the right friends has opened many doors for me. Friendship is a process of osmosis – of giving and receiving. Some people may flatter you and send you flowers, but they are actually serving their own agenda, to benefit themselves. My father often said, 'Don't judge people by their flattering comments, only by their actions.' And it is only later on, when you have reached an advanced age, that you can really see who the people are who love you. One of the countless blessings of life is to love and be loved. That is a precious gift.

Some of the friends on my personal Roll of Honour are no longer with us. They include Peter Taylor, the Lord Chief Justice. He was the son of immigrant Jewish parents who originally settled in Leeds, and he rose through talent, intelligence and hard work to become the highest legal authority in the land. He gained a reputation as a fine judge: he campaigned for harsher sentences for drunk drivers who kill, and supported victims of domestic violence in their quest for justice. He had been the prosecuting counsel in Jeremy Thorpe's murder trial, although we didn't know that when we first met him, and he went on to undertake the inquiry into the Hillsborough football disaster. Peter loved music passionately, and was a good amateur pianist. One time he was on circuit at Leeds Crown Court. He rang up to invite us for dinner at the Judge's Lodgings. He and Geoffrey stayed up until 2 a.m. telling Jewish jokes. He said that it was delightful to have us as guests, because we were 'both such good value', and 'neither of us was a bore'. We were subsequently invited to stay with Peter and his wife at their home in Newcastle, and they came and stayed with us in Leeds. Peter was wonderful – he went round and chatted to everyone who came for dinner. He was very friendly and not at all stand-offish. He gave a speech at the 1993 Leeds Competition, in which he said:

> The competition is in its thirtieth year, and, as has been said, it is a wonderful artistic event. It seems that the whole of Leeds has volunteered, or, by Fanny, been conscripted, to produce this civic phenomenon, but for all this the apex is one human dynamo. Fanny inspires and fires the competition with her own enthusiasm, verve and authority.

In 1995 Peter and I were asked by Sir Christopher Walford, then the Lord Mayor of London, to give a two-piano recital at a charity event in aid of the British Heart Foundation at the Queen's House in Greenwich. That was my first return to the concert platform for many years, and it raised a very large amount of money: £500,000. I told Peter it was entirely because everyone had wanted to come to hear the Lord Chief Justice play! It was so successful that we were asked to give another recital in Geneva not long afterwards, but Peter didn't return my phone call. When I called him again he broke the news that he had just been diagnosed with inoperable cancer, and retired shortly afterwards. He died of a brain tumour in 1997.

It was through Peter that I met another of the competition's staunch supporters, Harvey McGregor. Harvey was one of the finest lawyers in the country, an internationally renowned legal expert on damages, and a former Warden of New College Oxford. I nick-named him 'President of the Name-Dropping Society'. He was even worse than me in that respect! He told a story about how one day he had a phone call from the Foreign Office to say that the King of Spain had been awarded an honorary degree from Oxford University, and would it be possible for the king's helicopter to land in the grounds of New College? Harvey said, 'Certainly', and a few days later he was invited to attend the ceremonial dinner because of his kindness. When he asked his secretary to check his diary, she said, 'I'm sorry, but you can't do that date. You are dining with the Emperor of Japan!' Harvey could always trump anyone's card. He once invited Geoffrey and myself and Peter Taylor to stay at New College. One night Peter and I were giving a two-piano recital before dinner. The doorbell rang, and Harvey went down to answer the door. He came back just as the soufflé was rising for supper, saying airily, 'The Duke of Kent has just arrived, but he was an hour too early, so I sent him away and told him to come back later!'

Joan Valentine, my childhood friend and mentor, was closely involved with the behind-the-scenes arrangements at the competition until she retired in 1984. Although she had a high-powered professional job as Head of St John's College in York, no task connected with the Competition was beneath her dignity, down to the most menial administrative ones, such as sticking stamps on envelopes. She remained one of my closest friends until her death in August 2008 at the age of ninety-one. And on 6 March 2014 we lost Marion, at the age of eighty-seven. Three competitions ago Marion couldn't come up to Leeds because she had suffered a stroke, and was confined to a wheelchair. We all lived in hope that somehow she would get better, but she didn't. The last time I visited her, I knew I wouldn't see her again. She was noble, she was beautiful, she was perfect in life and was my best friend. Her light may have gone out, but she is cherished by her friends who will remember her for ever.

Through my work I have been privileged to come into contact with many great musicians. One of the most memorable was Mstislav Rostropovich. He was a larger-than-life character with a great sense of humour. I remember once being at Aldeburgh where Rostropovich was due to give a recital, accompanied by Murray Perahia. At the last moment, he announced that he was unable to perform due to illness, but was sending a pupil to give the recital in his stead. On to the platform came the female 're-placement', wearing a large-brimmed hat and a women's blouse. Geoffrey wasn't fooled for a moment. 'That's not a replacement,' he whispered to me. 'That's Rostropovich!'

Rostropovich could be rather manipulative. I remember the phone ringing one day. I picked it up and a voice on the other end said, 'Fanushka!' 'Who is speaking?' I said. 'It's Slava!' 'Slava who?' 'It's Slava Rostropovich here. I would like you to teach a young friend of mine, called Sara Wolfenson.' As soon as I heard the name, I knew straight away that Sara's father was President of the World Bank, and that Rostropovich, Nathan Milstein and Isaac Stern were trying to raise the money to restore Carnegie Hall. Another day he rang up and said, 'The daughter of a friend of mine has just arrived from America, and I'd like to send her up to Leeds now because I'd like your opinion of her playing.' I said, 'But surely she'll be suffering from jetlag?' 'No, it will be fine.' While I was listening to the girl play, the doorbell rang, and there on the doorstep was Clive Wilson from the Harrogate Festival, with a large carrier bag. The night before, Slava had been playing at the Festival and they had all been out for a drink afterwards. They had been drinking whisky in shot glasses, and Slava got it into his head that he must have some shot glasses for his flat in Paris. So poor Clive had to run all round Yorkshire trying to find out where to buy them. He now had a bagful, and the girl I had been asked to teach was being used as a courier to take the glasses back with her – it turned out she had been given the money to pay for them!

I keep in touch with my former pupil John Dyson, now Lord Dyson. I always knew he would do very well in life, not because he was by any means the best pianist I'd taught, but because he always prepared his lessons so thoroughly. Even when he was thirteen, he was meticulous in his preparation and examination of the musical score – it stood him in good stead for his work in the legal profession later on. I said to Geoffrey, 'The child is father to the man', as Wordsworth wrote. Learning an instrument is such a marvellous preparation for life, whatever you do. I could see where John was heading, and was not at all surprised when in 2012 he was appointed Master of the Rolls and Head of Civil Justice, which is the second highest legal position in the country. But he has never changed, and at heart he is still the John Dyson I knew when he was my thirteen-year-old pupil, now a very modest man.

My close friends now include some people who have helped the competition in many ways – such as the businessman and entrepreneur Sir Terry Bramall and his wife Liz, Keith and Pat Howard, Jeremy and Martine Burton and Marjorie Ziff, whose husband Arnold died in 2004. He was a businessman and philanthropist who made many gifts to Leeds, not just to our competition. The building that houses student services in the University is named after Marjorie and Arnold, and he donated generously to Jewish welfare organisations, as well as to Leeds Paris Church. Iris Haller, who has just celebrated her centenary, has been a lifelong friend, as are Anita Woolman, Françoise

Logan, and Betty and Leo Gruss. Betty and Hymie Marcus gave me so much support during Geoffrey's final illness and Dr Ingrid Roscoe, the first lady Lord-Lieutenant of West Yorkshire, has been a great help and support in recent years, as has Sir David Tang.

I have had some remarkable help from my 'team' since Geoffrey is no longer here. They include Cyril Stern, my driver; Linda Wellings, a counsellor and nurse who looks after and travels with me; Alan Stephenson, who knows as much about the competition as anyone I know, and helps with my correspondence and administration; Phillip Robinson, my financial adviser, my hairdresser Richard Mann, and my physician Dr Danny Hurwitz, who visits me regularly and takes a great interest in my comings and goings. Often, after we have chatted for some time and he is about to leave, he will say, as an afterthought, 'Oh, I forgot to ask. How are you?'

To these I would add another lifelong friend, Karin Pfautsch. Karin, who is German, came to us originally as our sons' nanny. After Geoffrey's death she has accompanied me on many foreign trips to sit on competition juries. If ever I am troubled, my first thought is to ring Karin, and she catches the next plane from Frankfurt to Leeds. Then there is my 'treasure', Trish, whose lovely smile brightens my days, and who exemplifies one of my favourite maxims: 'Whatever you do, you do to the best of your ability.' The unflinching love and support of all these people have made it possible for me to continue my work well into my tenth decade.

Although I was brought up in the Jewish tradition, Geoffrey and I were never religiously observant during our married life. Geoffrey, being a doctor and a scientist, resolutely refused to believe in God, and our children had a secular upbringing. Nevertheless, I am very proud of my Jewish identity, and my son Paul has become religiously observant in the Hassidic tradition. Many of the world's greatest pianists, violinists and conductors have been Jewish – such immortal names as Georg Solti, Mischa Elman, Artur Rubinstein, Emil Gilels, Yehudi Menuhin, Shura Cherkassky, Vladimir Ashkenazy, Daniel Barenboim, Vladimir Horowitz, Nathan Milstein, Ida Haendel, David Oistrakh and

Isaac Stern – and it is something to be proud of, especially as so many of them were born, like my own forebears, in Russia, and especially in Ukraine.

A reporter on a national paper once asked me, 'How is it, given your background, that you now move in such different social circles from where you started?' I replied, 'I can't tell you, it's very difficult to say. I always wanted to be popular, even as a child, and although I have a reputation for speaking my mind, people do seem to like and trust me, because I am never economical with the truth, and I have tried to be helpful to others in need. I say what I mean, and I mean what I say. People know where they stand with me. And I've never lost my sense of fun, and I've never changed my Yorkshire accent. I'm still just as I was.'

18

NINETY-FIVE YEARS YOUNG

How to make a day last an eternity?
Sunset and sunrise mark the rhythmical swing of my everyday life. In those half-waking moments before slumber overtakes me, I recall the achievements of the previous day, and anticipate what I must carry forward to the next. Every second of life has been precious to me, and I have not yet reached my destination.

I am no longer counting the years of my age. I prefer to follow Lord Chesterfield's words of advice to his son: 'I recommend you to take care of the minutes, for the hours will take care of themselves.' If you think about how many seasons there are in a year (4), how many months (12), then how many weeks (52), days (365), hours (8,760), minutes (525,949), and finally how many seconds (31,556,940), you realise that life is divided into millions of seamless segments, and you can use every one of them. I'm looking forward to the next stage in my life.

On 17 December 2014 I made this announcement in the press:

> I look back with pride at the international eminence the Competition has achieved over the past half century. The 'cottage industry' we dreamed up in 1961 has become, as Denis Healey, former Chancellor of the Exchequer, said, 'one of the musical wonders of the world'.
>
> The Leeds has achieved its renowned status and reputation through its musical integrity, and I am very grateful to the excellent competitors, juries, conductors, orchestras, friends, benefactors and volunteers whose contribution is everything.

Our Competition has introduced to the world some of the greatest pianists of our time and they carry our banner in international concert halls throughout the world, wherever they perform.

I feel ready now, after the 2015 Competition, to hand over the reins, in the hope that it will continue to thrive and grow, offering a platform of opportunities for young pianists, music lovers and audiences long into the future.

I was touched by the many tributes I received after announcing my retirement as Chairman and Artistic Director, but particularly this from Peter Donohoe:

More than anything, she has put the city of Leeds on the world's musical map . . . No one in musical history has achieved anything like what she has done, and the nation should be – and actually is – very proud of such an achievement.

The 2015 competition – our Golden Jubilee – will be a very special one. In March I attended a reception at the House of Lords in honour of my ninety-fifth birthday, and to launch my future initiatives. It was hosted by Baroness Deech, former Principal of St Anne's College, Oxford, and a pro-Vice Chancellor, as well as a distinguished law professor and Chair of the Bar Standards Board. She wrote an online blog afterwards, of which these are extracts:

Today Dame Fanny Waterman celebrates her ninety-fifth birthday. I was privileged to host a reception for her at the House of Lords a few days ago to mark her birthday, and to celebrate the Golden Anniversary of the Leeds International Piano Competition, which she founded, and which will be held again in September of this year. Among its award winners are Michael Roll, Mitsuko Uchida, András Schiff, Murray Perahia and Radu Lupu, and one may safely say that it is among the leading piano competitions in the world . . .

It put Leeds on the cultural map and has made an exceptional contribution to the musical life of the UK ...

So the story goes, one night in the early 1960s she woke her husband to say she had an idea, namely to start a leading piano competition to discover new talent. He told her to go back to sleep, but it was no dream, and she put her immense energy, charisma, organisational and fundraising skills to its establishment. Aung San Suu Kyi is a fan and asked to meet her when she was over here. Dame Fanny is retiring from the chairmanship, but, with her, 'retirement' has a nuanced meaning and she will be on hand for the recruitment of her successor. The competition is renowned for its integrity and thoroughness and looks set to continue for another fifty years ... Dame Fanny, a bundle of energy and shrewdness, is a star in Leeds, and has honorary doctorates from Leeds and York (why not Oxford and Cambridge?). Fortunately, musicians seem to live for longer – there is clearly a life force in music.

The Lord Mayor of Leeds wrote:

Dear Dame Fanny

On behalf of the City of Leeds, I would like to take this opportunity of congratulating you on your ninety-fifth birthday on 22 March. Over the years you have touched the lives of many with your musical talent, as well as creating a competition with a worldwide reputation.

I know that this is a very special and poignant year for you, and it therefore seems appropriate at this time to add that Leeds is proud of all your achievements and that you remain one of the City's greatest ambassadors.

And Graham Johnson, one of our most distinguished musicians, wrote to me on the occasion of my ninety-fifth birthday while thanking me for my comments on a recent Schubert broadcast. His words echo my ethos and responsibility as a musician to the art of music, and my own fears for its future:

This grateful message comes with my belated warmest wishes for your recent birthday on 22 March. I can think of no one better in English music whose values regarding playing and serving the composers are those by which we should continue to live. But I do fear for the future, Dame Fanny. Years ago, real shops were replaced by self-service supermarkets. These days, real pianists are replaced by self-serving super-egos. The result is that everything sounds as if it has been snatched off the shelf. I think that humility is one of the greatest virtues when one stands before a great piece of music – and you are a shining example.

I think often of another of Lord Chesterfield's pieces of advice: 'Firmness of purpose is one of the most necessary sinews of character, and one of the best instruments of success. Without it, genius wastes its efforts in a maze of inconsistencies.' I deplore the modern mania for constant change and dumbing down. I strongly believe in the old traditions, but also, one must be aware of positive developments and improvements.

I am determined to go on looking forward. I still have a great deal of energy and imagination, and a thirst for new projects. At present I am as busy – or even busier – than I have ever been. In addition to my teaching, I have this spring been filtering the largest number of entries for the competition that we have ever had – over four hundred. The competitors are not entering for the money prizes but for the opportunities we offer – our priceless list of winners' engagements. Ben Frith and Jonathan Dunsby have been sitting with me from ten in the morning until ten at night, listening to the tapes and videos sent in by hopeful entrants. We three have listened to every note of every bar of every piece, and consider carefully before making any decision about acceptance or rejection. I chose Ben and Jonathan to help me because they are absolutely honest, and I know that we are all in accord as to what qualities we are listening for. We are looking for what I call the 'Leeds Brand'. Because of the way I play, the way I teach, and my admiration for the great pianists past and present, we are looking for that special kind of artist who will continue the high standards of our previous prize-winners, carrying the banner of the Leeds all over the world. Almost every day when I'm listening to the radio, I hear that 'So-and-so won the Leeds International Piano Competition'. My brand and my choice of competitors have ensured that the competition is recognised by the international music community as the Gold Standard of music competitions. And that is what I hope to hand on to my successors.

This will be our eighteenth competition. Some things have changed over the years since we started our 'cottage industry' – the competition now spreads over three weeks, rather than the original two, and there is greater free choice of repertoire. But we still believe that the test of a fine pianist is how they perform works by the great masters, and the first-stage programme must include a piece by the composers who have always stood at the heart of the Leeds Competition – Bach, Mozart, Haydn and Beethoven. And Benjamin Britten's *Notturno* remains a compulsory piece in the semi-final stage.

The BBC is once again playing a major role in disseminating the competition to a worldwide audience through its broadcasts on Radio 3 and on BBC4 television. I am particularly pleased that two outstanding competitors from 2012 – our Swiss runner-up Louis Schwizgebel, and Chinese semi-finalist Zhang Zuo – have been selected to take part in the BBC's prestigious New Generation Artists scheme.

The nationalities of the competitors have changed a great deal, with many more coming from the Far East and from all corners of Europe. This was not the case back in 1963, at the height of the Cold War, when the majority of the entrants were British. The number of British entrants has declined over recent years, but I am so pleased that this year there are four excellent British pianists entering the Leeds, and I hope the tide has turned.

As always, the competition is receiving financial support from Leeds City Council, and the invaluable practical support of the University. Without the help of these two institutions, the Leeds could never have flourished. As we no longer have a major single sponsor, we have to rely on a growing list of help from private trusts and foundations, commercial companies and generous individual benefactors, including the Friends of the Leeds International Piano Competition, the Liz and Terry Bramall Charitable Trust, the Emerald Trust Foundation, Marjorie Ziff, Robert Tebb, Sir David Tang and others. Our prize-fund now totals over £70,000, and in addition, the Terence Judd–Hallé Orchestra Prize of £5,500, plus at least three paid engagements with the Hallé, will be once more offered to a finalist chosen by the orchestra members. That prize is sponsored, most generously, by the Hallé under its conductor Sir Mark Elder, together with my former pupil Jonathan Moulds.

For our Golden Jubilee, we are receiving a generous donation from the Sir Jack Lyons Charitable Trust – our first sponsors back in 1963 – in memory of Roslyn Lyons. It will be used to sponsor a series of five debut recitals by some of our prizewinners at the Wigmore Hall. And I am delighted and honoured that our Global Ambassador, Lang Lang, the most celebrated pianist in the world, is visiting Leeds this September to offer his services in aid of the competition.

Since 2003 we have also been very pleased to have practical support for the competition from Steinway & Sons. That year they donated twenty-four pianos, which were installed in private homes all over the city for the competitors to practise on, and were later auctioned to raise money for the 2006 competition. In 2012 Steinway delivered twenty grand pianos on loan to Leeds piano hosts, and also installed a special pair of Steinways in the University's Great Hall and at the Town Hall.

The distinguished jury for the 2015 competition includes three former Leeds competitors: Pascal Devoyon, who came joint third with András Schiff in 1975, Boris Petrushansky and Anne Queffélec, who came fourth and fifth respectively in 1969. Other pianist members of the 2015 jury will include Nikolai Demidenko from Russia, Eleanor Wong from Hong Kong, Marios Papadopoulos from Cyprus, Tong-il Han from South Korea, who was the first Korean pianist to play with the major international orchestras; and Jerome Lowenthal and Robert MacDonald from the USA.

Adam Gatehouse, who formerly ran the New Generation Artists programme at BBC Radio 3, returns for a second time, and we have invited Daniel Evans, Artist Manager at the New York-based CAMI agency.

One of the great successes of the Leeds Competition is that I have always paid great attention to the smallest detail. As Nadia Boulanger said, one must devote the same amount of care to the most menial task, as to the greatest. We are already planning menus for the jury and for the competitors, who since 2009 have been accommodated at the University's Devonshire Hall. The arrangements are managed by Beverley Kenny and overseen by one of our Executive Trustees, Telsa Woolman, who has a team of volunteers under her.

Looking back to our first competition in 1963 makes me realise just what a 'cottage industry' it had been, in comparison with today. Then, we had just one car available to ferry competitors around – now, we can muster nearly fifty drivers, as well as about forty-five piano hosts. Many people give up their time generously to help as stewards at the Great Hall and Town Hall. They are all vital to the success of the competition, and are irreplaceable. The volunteers who help and direct the competitors before they walk on to the platform are particularly important – they should be quietly spoken and reassuring. The important role once fulfilled by Geoffrey – that of announcing the competitors as they walk on to the platform – is now taken by another doctor, the eminent cardiologist Professor Lip-Bun Tan, who has worked as a consultant at the Leeds Teaching Hospital Trust.

During the competition a daily programme is drawn up, and all the music being played is laid out on tables for the jury, in the correct order of playing. We try to ensure that the seats for the jury are comfortable, and have armrests, as the jury members will be sitting on them for ten hours a day.

I only wish that we could recapture the selfless spirit and family atmosphere of our first great committee, who gave generously of their time, their wisdom and their energy without counting the personal cost. We were a family.

Meanwhile, in my ninety-sixth year, I am focusing my mind on two exciting new initiatives. I am greatly concerned by the noticeable diminution of audiences for classical music. Audiences now consist of mainly elderly people, and without younger listeners, classical music will wither and venues will close. I am Chairman of the Yorkshire and Humberside branch of the *Live Music Now!* Scheme, which aims to take live music, often played by young performers, into schools, hospitals and prisons; and in addition, I am planning a new venture to help disadvantaged children from a very early age to learn to love music. I believe that young children should be taken to concert halls to hear orchestras being rehearsed by great conductors. This should be an enjoyable event for them, and an excellent communicator, someone such as Howard Goodall or Douglas Scarfe, could introduce them to music and inspire a passion for it, so that it becomes a primary force in their lives. I am being supported in my efforts in this project, *Young Audiences*, by my very good friends Sarah and David Kowitz, who will be joint chairmen with me, and Lady Valerie Solti, who is devoting a great deal of time and effort to the promotion of music among the young.

Secondly, since major competitions usually take place in a capital city, such as Moscow, Warsaw, or Brussels, I am interested in the possibility of building up musical links between Leeds and London. The resources available to London offer so much potential. In 1963, when people asked me, 'Where is Leeds?' I would say, 'Well, it's an industrial city in the North of England', and they would look blank. London, however, is one of the greatest musical, educational and cultural centres in the world, and Leeds could only benefit from closer links with the capital.

I am also looking forward to continuing my association with the Harrogate Festival. I have been a member of its governing body for the past twenty-five years, and in 2009 I was invited by its dynamic Chief Executive, Sharon Canavar, to become its President. Yorkshire sorely needs a good music festival since the demise of the Leeds Triennial Festival, which was once associated with such great conductors as Thomas Beecham, Malcolm Sargent and Carlo Maria Giulini, and hosted the premieres of wonderful works such as Elgar's *Caractacus* and Walton's *Belshazzar's Feast*. That festival has not survived the present age of austerity. Not long before its collapse I warned its Artistic Director, Alexander Goehr, about his programming policy. 'Sandy,' I said, 'you are putting too much emphasis on contemporary music for the tastes of our Leeds audiences.' 'My job is not to put bums on seats,' he replied. I strongly disagreed with him, and the festival disintegrated as audiences deserted it. The Harrogate Festival, a relative newcomer which celebrates its fiftieth anniversary in 2015, has on the other hand chosen to evolve and thrive. It has branched out to accommodate disciplines other than music, and now aims to deliver a year-round programme of arts and cultural activities. I think its strong educational bias is particularly commendable. There is now a Literature Festival, a Crime Writing Festival, a History Festival and a Children's Festival, as well as a Music Festival, which offers a series of Sunday morning coffee concerts in the Old Swan Hotel. They are a real treat, and a great success.

Music is the greatest bonding factor. I believe firmly that, perhaps more than anything else, it can break down cultural barriers between nations and open the gates of the world. This year the theme of the Harrogate Festival, 'A Sense of Place', aims to bridge the divide between Arab and Jewish communities in Israel – something that Daniel Barenboim has worked so tirelessly to promote. Its schedule includes a lecture by Alfred Brendel as well as concerts by the Polyphony Foundation under their director Saleem Ashkar. At one of my recent musical evenings my guests included the Archbishop of York, Dr John Sentamu and his wife, Margaret. I said to Dr Sentamu, 'Don't you think that politics and religion too often divide, whereas music unites?' I've seen the power of *die holde Kunst* – 'the heavenly art' – and how it works.

My own life's work serving the cause of music has been an honour, a passion and a privilege. Five years ago I was awarded Honorary Membership of the Royal Philharmonic Society. The Council's Citation was read by its Chairman, John Gilhooly:

Over the years, several very distinguished pianists have received Honorary Membership of the Royal Philharmonic Society: Ignaz Paderewski, Clara Schumann, Solomon, Gerald Moore, Claudio Arrau and Graham Johnson to name but a few. But arguably none has done so much to further the cause of the piano and piano playing as the indefatigable powerhouse that is Fanny Waterman.

Both as a concert pianist and later as a teacher, Fanny is led by her passion for music and rigorously high standards. Her status as a teacher is now legendary: she has inspired and instructed generations of musicians, both in person and through the millions of copies of her teaching books sold around the world.

Fifty years ago, together with Marion Thorpe and her late husband, Dr Geoffrey de Keyser, she founded the Leeds International Piano Competition in her beloved Yorkshire, with which her name has become synonymous. She has nurtured it into one of the greatest international piano competitions in the world and launched the careers of such virtuosic young pianists as Radu Lupu, Murray Perahia, Mitsuko Uchida and András Schiff.

That seems to me to sum up what I have tried to achieve.